I0133198

Break FREE

12 Scientifically Proven Ways to Be Incredibly Happy

Soft Cover Edition
October 1, 2014

By
Dr. Jill Ammon-Wexler
http://www.BuildMindPower.com

Dr. Jill Ammon-Wexler

ISBN-13: 978-0991037940
ISBN-10: 0991037944

SOFT COVER EDITION

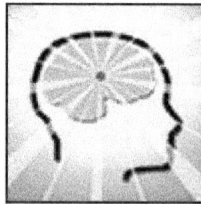

Published by
Quantum Self Group, Inc
217 Cedar Street #268
Sandpoint, Idaho 83864 USA

CONTENTS

Dr. Jill Ammon-Wexler

INTRODUCTION

How is it that some people manage to suddenly transform their lives seemingly overnight? Let's look at the mystery of personal transformation from the brain-out. Everything we do, or even think of doing, all begins in the same place – as a very real spark of electro-chemical energy in our brain.

You can suddenly make a decision to change the way you respond to those sparks and you transform your entire reality – including your energy, your charisma, your relationships, your health, your success, your happiness and your entire future.

This insight is the direct opposite of the popular assumption that our lives are controlled by forces outside of ourselves. Yes, we are certainly influenced by what's happening around us. BUT...

It really IS true that the greatest journey starts with the first step, and that first step starts with a decision. This book is designed as that step – the insights you'll encounter will trigger immediate changes in how you feel about who you are, and who you are becoming.

I have included some stories of real people and explanations of important research studies to help you build your belief and understanding that YOU TOO can do this.

Whether your ultimate goal is to climb the corporate ladder at work, start your own business, improve your health, or even develop your ESP powers – it all starts with a simple decision. Then your goal is to reach into your own brain and replace any self-limiting beliefs, assumptions and habits that might have been holding you back.

The methods in this book are based on the same techniques and insights I have shared for over 45 years with my personal clients from around the world. They work. Apply the insights in this book and they will work for YOU too.

With my sincere best wishes for your expanded confidence, motivation and happiness. Enjoy!

Dr. Jill

WHAT'S INSIDE

Discover the TRUTH about what's TRULY possible for you based on the latest scientific research. This is guaranteed to shock any idea of having "personal limitations" right out of your mind.

Get ABSOLUTE CLARITY on exactly how you continuously create your own reality from the brain out – and how to immediately take charge of that important creative process.

EXPAND your mind power. Take an exciting tour through your brain, how it works, and how to immediately begin to unfold your true natural mind power. Understanding this changes everything!

ELIMINATE negative thinking and rapidly overhaul your personal belief system.

TAKE ADVANTAGE of a tough childhood. Did you have a tough childhood? Learn why this can be a huge plus. Discover why being "realistic" about yourself and your potential is one of the worse things you can do! This scientific research will amaze you.

7

OVERCOME limiting beliefs. The beliefs stored in your subconscious mind control who you are and who you can become. Discover a proven-effective way to instantly overcome any limiting beliefs that are holding you back.

STOP the worry cycle. Ever notice that what you worry about often comes true? Learn how this works in your brain, and a fast way to stop the worry cycle cold.

UNLEASH your natural genius. There's now solid scientific proof that geniuses are not born -- they are made. Learn how to embrace your full range of intelligences, and instantly expand your brain power. Just understanding this can increase your IQ!

TURN ON the burn. One of the most powerful brain-based aspects of your personal power is emotion. You'll learn how to tap into and use the amazing power of emotion to get what you want in your life – fast!

ONE. WHO ARE YOU?

A muscular truck driver wrestles with the door – jammed shut from the high speed impact. Flames lick at back of the car. It will obviously be all over in a matter of seconds.

The young woman at the wheel is unconscious – a scarlet river of blood streams down her forehead. Her 3-year-old daughter is screaming and wildly pounding on the window.

A white haired woman leaps from an old Chevy Cavalier and bolts toward the wreck. She shoves the truck driver aside, grabs the edges of the twisted door, and with one heave pulls it free.

She grabs the little girl, the truck driver pulls the woman from behind the wheel, and the two dive into the ditch just as the twisted wreck explodes.

How did that 116 pound 74-year-old woman do what a strong 258 pound man in his prime couldn't do?

Dr. Jill Ammon-Wexler

Was it a miracle? Most would say so.

What is the strange power of our brains that permits us to do such impossible feats of courage and strength? And how does this transfer into our personal power, happiness and success?

What is Personal Power?

Is it true that *only* the lucky few will ever discover their true purpose and meaning of life? Will only these "lucky few" discover the power within to achieve the highest levels of personal or business success? That common assumption is a life destroyer.

Creating a more powerful, fulfilled version of yourself is not only possible -- it's entirely within your reach, and is far easier than you might think!

You CAN tap into and unfold your own personal purpose and passion, and that is exactly what this book is all about! You're capable of creating a whole new personal reality. Suddenly people and opportunities will seem to be drawn to you. Your old limitations begin to just fall away and success in any life venture will follow in your footsteps.

Does this sound impossible or, at the least, highly unlikely? Read on!The goal of this book is to reveal exactly how YOU can claim a more empowered, fulfilled and exciting version of yourself from the brain-out … expanding to claim more of your TRUE potential. Let's start with the stories of two *very real* people I know personally who did just this:

SOPHIE'S STORY begins at age six when her French grandmother told her of her grandfather's dream to leave France and go to America to build a better future for the family.

He never made it, as war claimed his life. But hearing his story was the beginning of Sophie's dream of leaving her home on a small South Pacific island to move to what she saw as the land of opportunity – America.

An adventurous soul, Sophie left home for Tahiti at 20. Her fate began to change just one short year later when one day a handsome young American came into the store where she worked. He was hoping to find someone who spoke English. Sophie came to his rescue, and they ended up dating.

"Just before he left two weeks later, I did a strange thing," Sophie recalls. "I just opened my mouth and told him I would come to America in one year to visit him. It wasn't a conscious plan – it just popped out."

Shortly after Sophie bought a book that would change her life – a guide to the powers of the mind.

"I came home every day from work and went straight for that book," she recalls. "Soon I wasn't concerned with how I was going to do it. I just *knew* I was going."

Eleven months later – one month from her target date for leaving – Sophie gave notice at work. Her final paycheck wasn't enough to buy a ticket to California. "But I still wasn't worried," she recalls.

Sophie described her challenge to a friend. He helped her get a discounted ticket to Hawaii, and even gave her the phone number of some of his friends in Los Angeles.

When Sophie arrived in Los Angeles she had $5 in her pocket, and still trusted the fates to provide for her. Sure enough, a couple on the plane bought her a motel room and fed her. The next day she called the number in LA and was again taken in and cared for.

"From the very beginning it all just happened with no effort or worry at all," she recalls. "Everything just came together and fell into my hands."

What enabled Sophie to soar so effortlessly through such a dramatic quantum leap? It all began with a decision.

But from the very beginning her decision went beyond goal setting – it was an absolute brain-based claim that a different reality BELONGED to her. She was going to America, her land of opportunity, on the announced date. Period. "How" was simply *not* an issue!

Sophie consistently claimed this reality as true without worrying about "how" it was going to happen. She constantly reminded herself that it belonged to her.

Sophie's life thereafter is filled with one miracle after another. She is today an extremely successful self-made entrepreneur, and "worry" and "how" are still not part of her vocabulary!

RALPH'S STORY. Ralph's story is quite different. Ralph had spent the night barely clinging to life as an unbelievably enormous amount of cocaine surged through his body. His heart had raced, stopped, and then started to pound wildly again. His cat sat on his chest all night staring at him – actually throwing him a life line.

Ralph was deeply hooked on cocaine, and had become a dealer to support his huge need for the drug. The night before he had tried to control himself by setting an egg timer to try to wait three minutes between lines. But he quickly quit using the timer and simply chopped and snorted one line after another – pausing in between only to slug down another huge glass of cheap red wine.

Ralph forced himself onto his feet that next morning to build a fire in the wood stove "Something had to happen," he recalls. "There was no doubt I was killing myself. I was drinking a large bottle of wine every day and not eating. And that morning I had blood in my urine, and coming out of my nose and ears."

What happened next had never been planned.

In a brief moment of life-affirming clarity, Ralph grabbed up what was left of almost a pound of cocaine and his kit and threw them into the fire. He then went to the phone and called his supplier and told him if he ever sold him more cocaine he would turn him in to the police. He then called his remaining three friends and told them the same thing.

The next three days were pure hell. "It was beyond withdrawal," he recalls. "It was a big blur ... I passed back and forth through death's door."

On the fourth morning Ralph took another quantum leap. "I felt like I needed to make a new commitment to life," he says. "The only thing I could think of was going to a gym to work out, and maybe getting some organic food and juice."

What happened from there?

One year later almost to the day Ralph participated in a local novice bodybuilding contest. He smiled when I asked him if he won. "I won in here," he beams, pointing to his heart. Incidentally Ralph, is today a very successful motivational coach. He brings an electrifying level of passion and clarity to his work, and has a very long list of clients.

Here's the interesting point about Sophie and Ralph. They each took immediate and irreversible action on a passionate decision. They didn't struggle to decide "how" to dramatically change their lives or create new business opportunities. They just took action!

How did they do this? They each made an <u>instant</u> decision, *committed* to it, and took consistent <u>action</u>. This is the MOST BASIC SECRET to making a RAPID change.

Can You Do This?

Could YOU do this? Most of us were taught that change is difficult, and takes struggle and long years to accomplish. But there's another type of personal change possible – the instant transformation that

Dr. Jill Ammon-Wexler

comes from making a passionate commitment and acting on it.

Sophie and Ralph shared the common source of all such dramatic personal changes -- a decisive personal commitment backed by action. They are each an example of how a focused mind and commitment can create instant and lasting positive change in YOUR life.

Such a change might be as dramatic as one day quitting your job and boarding a plane to create a new eco-business in the jungle of Costa Rica. Or it could be suddenly deciding to "make up" with an old friend, grabbing the phone to call them, and diving into a positive new relationship.

Over my years of working with world-class leaders in business, sports and the performing arts I've observed the power of a certain approach to creating a successful life. Here it is: The best way to achieve any goal is to BECOME the person that goal belongs to. The goal will then seem to simply drop into your hands effortlessly.

This book is a road map to unleashing your true inner power and powering up your self confidence – to stepping into an exciting new version of YOU!

What's required on your part? Just desire, commitment and action!

Where It All Starts

So, how is it possible to create a dramatically empowered new personal reality? The answer is sitting right there on your shoulders.

The potential for dramatic rapid personal development is naturally built right into your brain. But I'm not talking about just positive thinking, or the power of attraction, or manifestation, or visualization, or any of the other commonly recommended self-growth tools. And I'm not talking about struggling and endless effort to change either.

These are all incomplete by themselves!

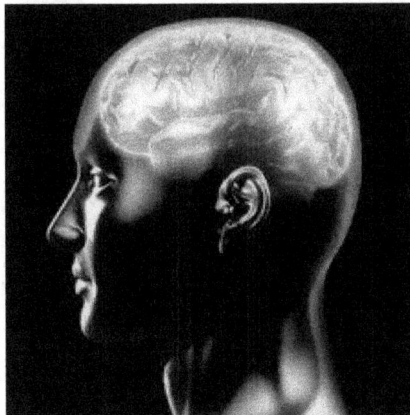

The source of who you are –
your amazing brain.

17

Dr. Jill Ammon-Wexler

Making a rapid positive change starts with understanding *exactly* how your brain creates your reality, and how you can effortlessly take over and direct that process. The goal of this book is to provide you with steps YOU can take to instantly make your personal life (and your business) a dramatically more exciting and successful place to be.

Your Natural Genius

Let's start at the *true* source of who you are – your unique physical brain. In terms of sheer power and intricacy, your brain leaves the greatest of today's computers far behind and choking in the dust.

Consider this: You have 30 billion (yes, *billion*) neurons in your brain. What are neurons? The powerhouse little cells that let your brain dream, plan, analyze, remember, and reach out to control literally every single cell in your body.

Plus ... consider that each of those tiny neurons is actually a miniature self-contained computer. Your brain is actually a supercharged marvel. It processes an estimated 30 billion bits of information every second.

But this gets even more amazing. Each of your brain cells can also communicate with thousands of other brain cells. Each one! And your brain contains 100,000 miles (yes, *miles*) of "communications cable" they use to talk back and forth among themselves.

If we were to stretch out the brain cells (neurons) from just your brain end to end, the line of neurons would actually stretch thousands of miles. This is *not* an exaggeration. It's a scientific fact. And all of this is packed into only 3+ pounds.

So here is an interesting question to consider: With all this amazing mental power, why don't we each have everything we want in life? Why can't we just shake off sadness and discouragement and stress and experience happiness? Why can't we easily change any behavior we want to change – or at least overcome our limiting thoughts? And why do so many businesses fail or just never reach their true potential?

It's NOT your fault if you haven't achieved your dreams, or feel like you can't get your life or business together. There really isn't anything wrong with you. You are NOT a failure, and you are not hopeless!

You're just stuck in a mental reality that's limiting who you can be! And the path to correcting that is NOT year after year of struggle and gradual growth.

Dr. Jill Ammon-Wexler

You have probably already tried that. The best answer is INSTANT transformation – literally claiming a new personal reality from the brain-out.

Is <u>Instant</u> Change Possible?

Modern science has proven that our brains constantly grow and change well into old age. In fact your brain is built to naturally thrive on challenge and change. Our brains are actually so changeable that the scientific world had to create a new term – "brain plasticity."

Today's high tech instruments actually let scientists watch as a single thought physically rewires our brains. This is real. And recent research has proven our brains automatically rewire themselves within hours following each new experience.

Why is this so important? It's important because we now have PROOF that each of your thoughts physically changes your brain INSTANTLY.The ability to re-create yourself and truly reach your dreams is right there within your physical brain – at this very moment.

Imagine what it would be like to rewire your brain to experience creativity like Leonardo da Vinci, to experience business clarity like Bill Gates, to tap into personal charisma like Oprah, or to experience the powerful mental focus of an elite athlete?

You will learn exactly how to do this as we go along. Success with this approach has little to do with efforting and struggling to "change." It simply requires opening your mind to certain truths ... then allowing your new reality to flow from those new insights.

The Nature of Change

Let's take a closer look at the nature of change and how it personally impacts YOU! On the most basic level, we are each active players in a dynamic, constantly changing quantum universe. Like everything else in the known universe, we are also constantly being transformed from matter to energy and back.

☆ **In fact – we literally ARE change! And YOU are NOT an exception.**

Dr. Jill Ammon-Wexler

TWO. YOUR AMAZING SELF

Is fire really hot? A few years back in California I saw a poster announcing a firewalk. I'd always wondered if fire walking was really real, so I decided to sign up.

But at about 10 o'clock the morning of the event I began to have second thoughts. I called to cancel. "Fear is a common part of the experience," the firewalk coordinator laughed. "And you may at well come, since we don't give refunds."

So I re-committed – thinking I could always just watch.

That evening my doubt came flooding back when I was presented with a firewalk liability release form. But I signed the form, and my companion and I joined the motley collection of people gathered in front of a giant canvas yurt. We were both immediately caught up in the nervous laughter rapidly spreading from person to person.

23

A young woman ushered us in, and I settled onto one of the huge pillows circling the yurt.

A fire walker in action

The energy changed abruptly as the chiropractor hosting the firewalk burst through the door. To say he broke the ice would be a ridiculous understatement. He immediately lit up the entire yurt with his remarkably contagious laughter.

After about an hour of storytelling, chanting, spontaneous dancing and bursts of laughter, he led us out into the night.

I swallowed hard at my first sight of the shimmering firewalk path. We gathered around the edges and watched six-inch tongues of fire leapt into the darkness as a young man walked along the edge of the 12-foot long bed of 1,400 degree Fahrenheit coals as he raked it.

The moment of truth had arrived. That fire pit looked as real as reality can get.

The chiropractor and his wife removed their shoes and socks and rolled up their jeans. I watched in disbelief as they clasped hands and calmly stepped onto the bed of red-hot coals. Sparks jumped from their feet as they walked the full length of the pit.

The chiropractor then invited the young man with the rake to be next, telling us he had walked on fire before. Seeing the young man literally dance the length of the pit was an amazing sight. Moments later the two people next to me stepped onto the coals, and I moved up to take my turn – barefoot and with my jeans rolled up to my knees.

Only half way across the firepit I felt a fist-sized coal brand itself into the outside of my right foot. I'll never forget the feeling as it hooked onto my flesh. But when I reached the end of the pit I realized I had no pain. I rubbed the side of my foot against the grass to remove the coal, and rejoined the line. I firewalked a second and third time.

Afterward the energy was very high as we gathered again in the yurt. But suddenly a young man just to

Dr. Jill Ammon-Wexler

my left began to moan. I was amazed to see huge red burn blisters suddenly appear on his feet and ankles.

The chiropractor was very calm. He asked all of us to simply visualize the blisters gone, based on our own lack of burns. I watched in amazement as the blisters on his feet began to disappear. Within minutes he had no burns at all.

We Create Our Reality

It's commonly assumed that what we call "reality" is beyond our personal ability to change. Reality is just reality, right?

Not so!

The old belief that we have no control over what we call "reality" has actually fallen to the dust. Modern quantum science now tells us that we each actively interact with the entire universe. And if you pay attention to what the scientists are now saying, it is also now clear that we each literally create our own version of reality.

How do we do this?

Knowing the real secret behind firewalking can dramatically change your life, even if you choose to never experience walking on fire. Why?

Because firewalking is a <u>direct demonstration</u> of how your thoughts truly <u>DO</u> create your reality.

What Scientists Say

You might wonder what the medical world says about firewalking. Doctor Ron Sato of Stanford University's Medical School, also the director of a major California burn treatment facility, has an interesting viewpoint.

Doctor Sato treats people who have *accidentally* stepped on glowing coals and been burned so severely they required skin grafts. When asked about those who firewalk without injury, Dr. Sato simply says, "There's no logical explanation."

Renowned Harvard-trained physician and medical researcher Dr. Andrew Weil agrees. Doctor Weil, who has investigated firewalking for many years says, "The mental state is the KEY variable in firewalking."

So, what really makes firewalking possible? Tolly Burkan, the "father" of modern firewalking, claimed that walking on fire literally *creates a change in your brain chemistry.*

Brain chemistry?

Your amazing 3-pound brain is actually a dynamic electro-chemical "factory." And it is here that you create and manage your personal interpretation of what we call reality. This is not to challenge the miracle of life – it is simply a different way of understanding what we call reality.

Do you doubt that just a thought can cause actual physical changes in your body? Then consider the result of a sexual fantasy – or notice what happens when you even think of eating a lemon. Did your mouth begin to water?

"Positive thinkers literally live in a different chemical environment than negative thinkers," pioneer firewalker Burkan explained. It all comes down to this: Firewalking is a direct demonstration of the power of a thought to create what we call reality. And yes, I'm talking about *YOUR* personal version of reality!

Is Anything Real?

Einstein started it. Now scientists around the world are telling us that nothing is truly solid and the universe is a dynamic, constantly changing and perhaps endless field of consciousness.

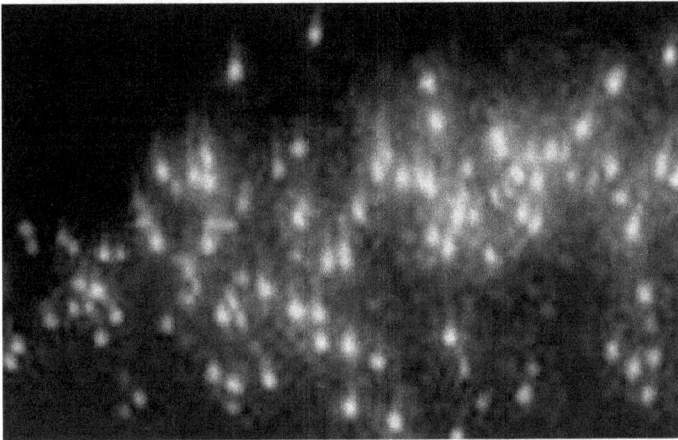

Electron photo of neurons firing
in the "Neuro-Universe" of your brain

So then … everything we assume to be real is actually information enclosed in tiny packets of a vibrating "something" that can change from matter to energy and back. And contrary to what seems to be so, our bodies and our brains are also absolutely *not* solid.

We are told the reason we cannot see everything as energy is because it vibrates too fast for our senses. But if we could see at the speed of light, we would

29

Dr. Jill Ammon-Wexler

look right into a vibrating quantum field capable of manifesting as either "physical" matter, or pure energy.

So it seems the so-called solid world exists only in our minds. You might even say we think the physical world into existence. And likewise through the amazing power of our thoughts, we also think our physical selves into existence.

What's the mystery behind all this? Scientists are now saying what mystics have claimed for centuries – that what we call "reality" is something of an illusion. But modern physics explains that this does NOT mean that nothing is real. Rather, we hold a learned shared illusion that what we see is what really exists.

In fact, some scientists are now telling us that at the very smallest of the small, there is not even energy anymore – the basic reality is a field of consciousness that we are all part of.

We are being told the real world is made up of a dynamic (and conscious) field that magically transforms into physical expression ... and that we each create our own version of it based on our own personal beliefs, expectations, and past history.

What's "Outside" You?

Can it really be true that we each CREATE our own version of reality?

That's an interesting question.

When you look out a window, it seems as though you are seeing an image of the outside world with your eyes. But we now know you do not really see the world with your eyes. What you actually see is a brain-created interpretation of the electrical signals passing through your eyes into your brain. This is not philosophical speculation – it is science-based reality.

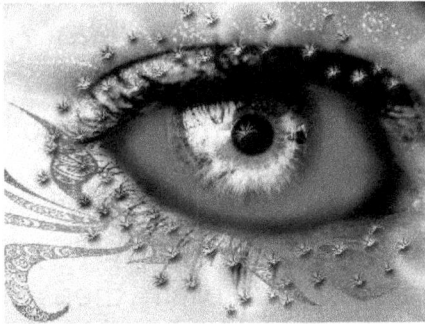

Here's how this works: The retinas of your eyes transform the light reflecting off an object into an electric signal that is sent into your brain. So your eyes really only see patterns of light.

Consider the page you are now reading: Your eyes send the light reflected off the page into your brain.

31

Dr. Jill Ammon-Wexler

Your brain then decodes the electric signals and creates a mental vision of the page. In other words, the words you are looking at are <u>not</u> outside you – they are actually inside you, in your brain's visual center.

Does this seem strange?

Well now it gets even more interesting. Notice the feel of the surface your hands are touching? It might seem normal to assume that surface or object is located outside of yourself. But this feeling is also created in your brain.

The nerves in your fingertips send electrical information to the tactile (feeling) center of your brain. And the sensation that anything is solid is also simply an *interpretation* that is wholly created by your brain.

Actually all impressions of the world enter your brain as electrical pulses. Your brain then compares them to past experiences for interpretation. And so, we create our sense of "reality" inside our own brains.

Applied to Your Goals

So how does all of this relate to a desire for something different in your life -- say a stronger self concept and a new level of happiness?

Your "happiness" is determined by what you visualize and desire – OR by what you fear and reject. Simply stated, it is your own creation. And all of this then guides the creation of your "reality."

Here's how this works: Let's take a look at what happiness really is. Viewed in scientific terms, happiness is a mental concept in your physical brain. I'm confident you can give an accurate definition of the word "happiness" without becoming emotionally involved.

But if I ask you, "What does happiness mean to you personally?"

Now suddenly everything changes!

In a millisecond your brain recalls your best friend in the 2nd grade comparing their family's new Cadillac to your family's beat-up Ford – or you remember wanting a new bike for Christmas, but being told to be realistic about your family's financial status. Or perhaps you were told as a child that you would never be "truly happy" unless you became a doctor or lawyer.

All of this is this stored deep in your subconscious mind. And unfortunately your subconscious mind does not respond to logical reasoning about how this old version of reality no longer applies to who you are today. So if your happiness falls short of your dreams, it is probably an old subconscious version of your reality holding you back. And here's the problem: Each time you revisit this old version of reality – the brain pathways holding it are physically strengthened.

This is not theory. This is hard, observable science. There's basically one way to overcome the subconscious stuff that keeps you from creating your ideal reality. You're going to have to reach in and reprogram your brain on a physical level.

How?

Build a Better Reality

Let's play with the fact that we live in a somewhat slippery and not really solid world ... and that our brain creates what we call reality. To do this we will start with the most basic reality creating tool of all – our thoughts.

Begin by allowing yourself to imagine your life as a MOVIE playing inside your brain. Because of the storage power of your subconscious mind, that movie contains everything that has ever happened to you, is happening to you now, and that could happen to you in the future.

So what?

Guess who is the STAR of the movie?

You are, of course!

And you are also the screenwriter, the camera operator, the producer and the director. Plus you are also the movie studio and the movie theater.

Rather, your brain is all of this!

☆ Actually what you call your "self" is a moving stream of images based on your memories of who you have been in the past, your sense of who you are today, and your vision of who you can become in the future.

Your brain continually rewrites and edits your movie, even when you are dreaming or daydreaming. And the great thing about this is the fact that YOU are in charge of the movie.

Dr. Jill Ammon-Wexler

Use Your Dreams

One very powerful way to begin to understand your personal movie is to pay attention to your dreams.

For much of history dreams were considered to be warnings of coming supernatural events, or even messages from the gods. But scientists now tell us that when we dream our brain is also busy organizing our memories.

Why is this important?

In many ways your sense of self is based on your personal storehouse of memories. Some psychologists actually claim we ARE our memories. And considering how those with Alzheimer's disease lose a sense of their own self, this does make sense.

Your dreams definitely do help write and revise the movie in your mind – your personal vision of reality and who you are. That is one of the reasons it is so rewarding to focus on your personal goals just before going to sleep.

Power of Daydreams

In many ways daydreams contribute even more to your internal movie than conscious thinking and analysis. Why? Because daydreams are actually a very powerful *future-creating process.*

This puts daydreaming into an entirely new light. Remember when you were in school and your teacher scolded you for daydreaming? Well guess what: A new University of British Columbia study has found that our brains are actually far more active when we daydream than previously thought.

The researchers found that the activity in several regions of our brain actually increases when our mind wanders. They also found the specific brain areas connected to solving a complex problem – previously thought to be dormant – are highly active while we daydream.

"Mind wandering is typically associated with negative things like laziness or inattentiveness," Professor Kalina Christoff of UBC says. "But this study shows our brains are very active when we daydream … much more active than when we focus on routine tasks."

The study had subjects perform a simple task of pushing a button when numbers appeared on a screen. The researchers tracked their attentiveness using brain scans, subjective reports from the subjects, and by tracking their actual performance on the task.

The conclusion? Daydreaming, which often occupies as much as one third of our waking lives, is a

Dr. Jill Ammon-Wexler

surprisingly important cognitive state during which we unconsciously sort through the important problems we face.

☆ So do you daydream of being a great actor, a Fortune 500 executive, a champion athlete, a best-selling author? Begin to pay attention to your daydreams to discover your true passions. Then commit to create what you dream of.

Feed Your Passion. Your daydreams actually rehearse the movie of your potential future reality. So here's something that is very, very important to remember: Your subconscious mind views daydreams as totally *real*. It is <u>not</u> able to tell the difference between your "real life" movie script, and your "daydream" movie script. This is very, very powerful in terms of re-creating your self esteem and confidence, and in changing your life for the better from the brain-out.

☆ The more focused quality time you spend "daydreaming" or "envisioning" exactly how you want your future life to unfold, the better that reality will settle into your physical brain. This takes visualization to the level of physical brain reality!

Here's something you will be learning more about as we go along: Your emotions have a very special power over who you will become. When you add passionate desire and intense emotion to your daydreams, your future movie becomes even more irresistible to your subconscious mind. You will then find yourself automatically taking actions you once thought were

Trust Your Intuition. Dr. Benjamin Spock told us, "You know more than you think you do." We come into life equipped with five basic senses – touch, hearing, taste, sight and smell. But many of us also possess some more mysterious senses like third eye vision, clairvoyance, and other related abilities.

One little understood sense – intuition – governs our ability to arrive at spontaneous gut-level decisions about our personal reality. The word intuition comes from the Latin word *intueri* -- to "look within." A good definition is, "the ability to have a complete understanding of something without logically analyzing it." In Japan, intuition is known as stomach art – an interesting turn on the Western "gut-level feeling."

Intuition is a unique whole brain function. It instantly ties together your higher mind, your entire lifetime of experience stored in your subconscious mind, and additional input from all five of your senses. And it does this in a millisecond – just another example of the amazing power of your brain.

39

Plus, because of the depth of knowledge your intuition taps into, it often provides insight into how you can instantly power-up your personal version of reality.

The secret is to begin to pay attention to your intuitive messages and insights that might come from your daydreams. And please remember, we are talking about the reality of how your physical brain is now known to work. This is not "pop" psychology, and it goes far beyond what you have learned in popular "self-help" books.

Do you have doubt about the practical value of intuition? Harvard researcher Jagdish Parikh studied 13,000 top business executives. He found that over 80% of them credit their business success to trusting their intuition.

Star in a Winning Movie

Is your personal reality less than a winning movie right now? Remember who is creating your reality? You! So why not write a new script for yourself and go to work directing a winner. All you have to lose are any self-created bad ratings.

Start with Passion. Choose your script carefully. For your dreams to manifest in your everyday life, you will have to really *want* them to do so. That is why it is so important to pick a script your innermost self really likes, and wants to play. Make sure your goals are absolutely based on your true passions. You want to choose a script that will create your ideal lifestyle – not something you don't really care about.

The more intense your passion for a new reality, the faster your brain will build new neural networks to support your desire.

Add Thought Power. Once you're certain you have picked a script you have genuine passion for, you will then want to be sure you play your role of director well.

A first-class award-winning movie (or life) does not just happen – it is the creation of a thoughtful, skilled Director. This is about designing and planning where your personal life is going. It's about creating a truly-desirable quantum leap landing point that will make your life movie a winner.

Take a moment to think about your life and who you want to be. This does not mean you have to be "possessed" thinking about the future. Just decide where you want to land.

Apply Intuition. Trust your intuitive intelligence. A major part of being able to soar through life is listening to what your deeper self is saying to you.

Dr. Jill Ammon-Wexler

We each have an intuitive internal wisdom and insight that can guide us onto an easier, far less stressful path to the life we want to be living.

This is NOT an esoteric notion – it's very real mind power in action.

You might want to reread this chapter and think about what it means to *CREATE* your own personal reality. This is the very core of personal power. Then create a script that defines WHO you want to be, and begin to put it into action.

THREE. WHAT'S GOING ON?

A Tibetan monk removes his distinctive burgundy and orange robes, folds them carefully, places them on a chair, and then slips into white "sweats" and throwaway paper slippers.

He shuffles down a long hall in the unfamiliar slippers and enters through an open door into a small windowless room. A doctor in a white medical coat looks up and smiles, then gestures toward a plush stuffed chair.

The monk nods and eases himself into the chair. The doctor skillfully inserts an IV into the monk's left forearm, and then gently wraps a suspended string around the monk's right index finger.

The monk has already received his instructions, and begins to relax into meditation as the doctor leaves the room. Minutes later the monk flexes his right index finger – pulling a cotton string to signal the doctor that he has reached the transcendental peak of meditation.

43

The doctor, Andrew Newberg, MD, immediately releases a radioactive dye into the IV line. Seconds later he is back in the room removing the IV from the monk's forearm. He immediately guides the monk into the next office.

Three minutes later the doctor is using a brain-imaging machine to see exactly which areas of the monk's brain were active when he achieved his transcendental peak.

Dr. Newberg has conducted high-tech brain research on meditating Tibetan monks and Franciscan nuns at prayer for some time. His work is typical of the amazing brain research being done today.

So do the monk's and nun's brains somehow change when they achieve their transcendental peaks? Dr. Newberg says "Yes." At the moment they have their remarkable "beyond time and space" sensations, measurable brain changes occur. At that point they have greatly reduced activity in the part of the brain that orients us in time and space – the "parietal lobe."

Newberg explains that this reduced brain activity shows that at the peak of their experience, the monks and nuns receive very little sensory data from outside their own self. He says this is what creates the sensation of "no time or space."

So we now know that the meditators' experience of being absorbed into a larger reality isn't imaginary. It springs from an actual brain state.

Enter "Inner Space"

Remarkable research is being done on the human brain today. Modern scientific technology now permits researchers to observe a healthy brain in action. This goes far beyond the former dependence on animal studies.

So – let's slide into our own inner space.

We now have measurable proof that thoughts have actual physical reality in the brain. One researcher has even pinpointed the exact spot in your brain that makes you a positive thinker – *IF* it is activated.

Ever wonder how your brain creates your awareness and lets you respond to what is happening around you? This question has echoed down through the ages – with thinkers proposing everything from a tiny man sitting inside your head, to something like physical gears and machinery.

But your brain is actually an amazing ultra high-tech 3-pound electrical and chemical biological "factory." We now know that your brain produces from 5 to 10 watts of very real and measurable electricity – enough to light up the inside of your refrigerator!

You learned years ago in school that your heart and all your other internal organs are made up of collections of specialized little biological marvels called cells. Well your brain is no exception. It is also a collection of special cells surrounded by a protective membrane – just like your heart, lungs, kidneys, and all of your other internal organs.

But let's skip unnecessary scientific stuff and go straight to where it all begins – your brilliant little brain cells.

Meet the Communicators

The cells in your brain have some fancy Latin names -- "neurons" and "glial cells." We will not be too concerned with the glial cells, since they are primarily the support and communication channel side of the team. Your neurons, on the other hand, are the thinking member of the team, so I will just refer to them as your "brain cells."

Those powerful little neurons create the 5 to 10 watts of electricity your brain generates. They are very excitable and talkative, and their basic job is to constantly send chemical messages back and forth among themselves.

These constant messages are at the core of your brain's ability to think, perceive and remember. They are also responsible for the biochemical signals that control your bodily functions.

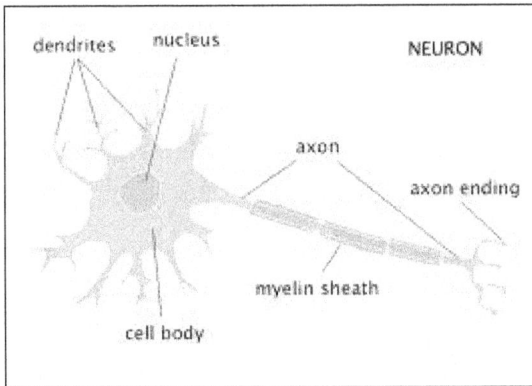

Your neurons are built for communication, and have branches and roots similar to trees. The branches (axons) carry messages to other brain cells. They function a lot like the electrical wiring in your house, and are even insulated.

47

Dr. Jill Ammon-Wexler

The roots (dendrites) receive messages carried by the axons of other brain cells.

How Your Brain Works

Let's add to the insights of how your amazing brain directs your behavior and creates your reality.

Your brain can just slide along on its own directing your behavior and responses, solving problems, and occasionally thinking its way out of a box. But what if you really understood how your brain works on a deep intuitive level. Your mental power could then expand to a supercharged level of performance.

Let's take a short tour of how your brain works: Imagine for a moment that it's a warm sunny day, and you're visiting the zoo with a friend. Suddenly the public address system orders all visitors to exit immediately.

It seems a tiger has escaped from its cage. You spin around looking for the nearest exit, and then spot two yellow eyes staring at you from behind a nearby bush.

Will I Survive? That vision of two golden tiger eyes roars into your brain demanding an immediate, emergency-level response. Your very survival could be at risk. So your vision of those golden eyes is sent straight to a specific part of your brain that's specifically dedicated to survival. In a millisecond you have landed in very special area of your brain stem called the Reticular Activating System (RAS).

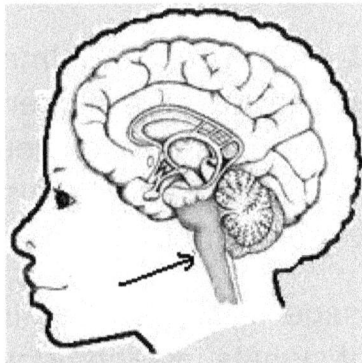

The brain stem connects your
brain and your spinal cord

The RAS is packed like a can of sardines with thousands of other sensory signals collected at the same time you saw those tiger eyes. There's the sound from the public announcement system, the scent of the nearby flowers, the feeling of your

Dr. Jill Ammon-Wexler

fingernails cutting into your palms, and a wrap-around kaleidoscope of other sensory impressions.

If you could look inside your RAS you would be able to watch as most of these sensory signals are immediately discarded. Why? Because your survival-oriented RAS automatically identifies the most important information, and just filters out the rest.

You can bet your RAS immediately focuses on the "I see a tiger" visual signal. Why? Because its job is to quickly identify anything important to your survival so it can immediately notify your higher brain centers of the need for rapid action.

What Should I Do? Your RAS immediately sends the tiger eyes image up to a higher brain center – your Limbic System. This part of your brain creates and deals with emotion, and is also tied to your memories, motivation, and thinking.

When the message reaches the limbic system a massive steam of signals instantly flows outward.

Your brain orders your blood pressure and heart rate to increase, your big muscles to contract, and stress hormones to flood into your blood stream. This is commonly referred to as the "stress response."

So now – only milliseconds after seeing those tiger eyes – you're totally prepared to either fight or run.

And all of this has happened before you even had time to think about what you should do.

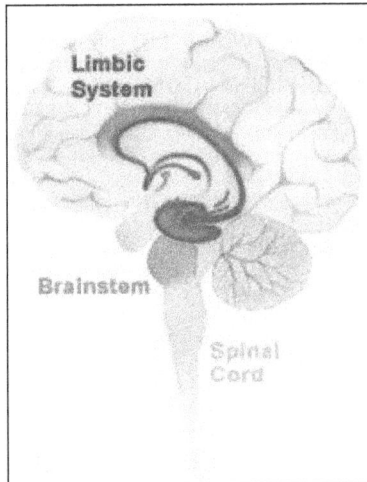

Is This My Best Response? A few milliseconds later all of this enters the major "thinking" part of your brain – your Cerebral Cortex. Your higher brain immediately realizes you responded to a false alarm, and sends this message down to your limbic system.

The limbic system has now been ordered to cancel your emergency response; but that will take some time since your body is now flooded with stress-related bio-chemicals.

Ever wonder why it's often so hard to control your emotions? Although emotion and thinking interact, they each have separate brain pathways. Emotions are difficult for the cortex (your thinking brain) to turn off for a physical reason:

(1) The connections coming down from your cortex to the limbic system (your emotional brain) are less well developed than the connections going up from the limbic system to the cortex.

(2)   So once an emotion has kicked in, your emotional brain (your limbic system) automatically has the upper hand over the cortex. It's all a matter of millisecond timing.

What Happened Was. When you later sit down with a friend over coffee and begin to tell her the story of what happened you then focus into a special part of your central brain – the Hypothalamus.

Your hypothalamus is actually your "memory secretary." All the details linked to seeing those tiger eyes were stored in your memory banks by the hypothalamus. And as you sit with your friend reviewing the event, your hypothalamus instantly reassembles all of the details together from their scattered storage places in your brain.

The feeling of the sun on your head and your fingernails cutting into your palms is pulled from your brain's "tactile storage center." The scent of the nearby lavender bush is pulled from your brain's "scent storage center." Everything you saw that was important is pulled from your brain's "visual storage center." And the sound of the PA messages is pulled from your brain's "auditory storage center."

The hypothalamus then presents all of this to you as a complete unified memory.

Develop Your Brain Power

Today's neuroscientists insist our brains have a high level of plasticity, and constantly change as they shape and re-shape our memories and experiences. We are being told this physically happens in our brain several times each day.

Researchers Henry Markram and Jean-Vincent Le Bé of France's Brain Mind Institute, for example, say the connections between our brain cells switch on and off very rapidly and are therefore constantly changing, strengthening and pruning our brain's circuitry.

"The circuitry of the brain is like a social network where brain cells are like people, directly linked to other people," explains Markram. "The brain is constantly switching alliances and linking with new 'circles of friends' to better process information."

Here's something to think about: Describing your brain's amazing potential is like trying to put your finger on a glob of mercury. Your brain contains a minimum of 1,000,000,000,000 individual neurons, and each of these cells can communicate with as many as +100,000 other neurons.

So how many brain cell-to-brain cell connections does your brain contain? If you were to write out the resulting number, the *number itself* would stretch over 10.5 million kilometers.

Transform Your Life Rapidly

Your brain pays closest attention to memories that are tied to strong emotions. Why? Because any thought or memory with a strong emotional charge automatically has a more complex (and durable) network of brain-cell-to-brain-cell connections.

Here's how this works: If you think something often enough with intense emotional feeling, that thought will create a stronger network of brain-cell-to-brain-cell connections.

While if you *stop* thinking about something (like a bad memory), the associated connections will begin to become less active and could eventually disappear entirely.

☆ There's something important to learn here. Since emotion strengthens brain connections, emotion is very important in making your life what you want it to be.

Put This to Work

Assuming you want to create a better lifestyle, Let's put some emotional power to work.

First. Select a primary goal. Make sure it is basically ONE goal, and not several all bunched together. You should be able to state it in 10 words or less. Suppose for our example that your goal is to "achieve prosperity."

Second. Next ask yourself questions like: "What IS prosperity (or happiness, or whatever it is you desire)? For example: Is prosperity a financial state, or does it have less to do with money, and more with something else? How would this look on a day-to-day basis? What do you have to do to make this be so?

Third. Now comes the emotional "juice" that will power your change: Make a genuine emotion-packed commitment to DO whatever it takes to achieve your goal. The more intense your emotional commitment, the faster you will get what you want. That's why it's so important to go after what you naturally feel passionate about.

Fourth. Now add the power of focused thought. This is where repetition enters in. You want to reprogram your brain to support what you DO want, and forget

what you do NOT want. Remember, your brain favors thoughts that are frequent or habitual.

Fifth. Here's a method that can move you along toward your goal: Every morning get a new 3 x 5 card and write a brief statement of your selected goal on it.

Then on the other side of the card write ONE specific thing you will do today to move closer to your end goal. This one thing must be real, specific, and achievable TODAY.

Put the card in your pocket or purse, and just DO that one thing by the end of the day. In only one month you will be astonished at how your life has changed.

FOUR. HOW WE CREATE REALITY

It is just after "reading time" in a Los Angeles second grade classroom. The attractive brunette teacher inserts a bookmark, closes her worn copy of "Alice in Wonderland," and gently places the book on her desk. As always after storytelling, her 23 young charges are attentive – waiting for their teacher's "story questions."

"What color do you think Alice's eyes were?" she asks the class.

Arms shoot up. The rapid-fire answers span every possible eye color – from blue to green to brown to black.

"Actually," she says, holding up the book, "you can see on the cover that Alice's eyes are blue. And here is what's so interesting about that. You know from the story that Alice is very curious and likes adventure. Right?"

Chirps of agreement come from the class.

57

"Well," she continues, "since Alice's eyes are blue, we know something very special about her." Keeping her agreement with a friend who is doing a post graduate psychology study, she then recites a script the psychologist provided: "Scientists did research that proved blue-eyed children are a lot smarter than brown- or green-eyed children. Isn't that interesting? So if you have blue eyes you are naturally smarter, just like Alice."

Do you remember how you trusted and admired your teachers as a young child? The students believed their teacher, of course.

The results were immediate and dramatic. The blue-eyed children immediately began to outperform their brown- and green-eyed classmates in all aspects of their studies.

The improvements continue until, one month later, the teacher announced that she made a mistake. She apologized, and said the study actually proved that brown- and green-eyed children are the most intelligent.

Again the results are dramatic and immediate. The blue-eyed children lost their edge and their performance dropped. The brown- and green-eyed children's grades, on the other hand, immediately soared to the superior range.

Incidentally, at the end of the test period the teacher does tell her students that the scientists were totally wrong – eye color is *not* an indicator of intelligence. *The children's performance then quickly returned to pre-experiment levels, regardless of their eye color.*

Interesting?

What Does This Mean?

Have you ever noticed that some of your habits and behaviors seem totally beyond your control and impossible to change, no matter how hard you try? Is this somehow the result of the structure of your brain? Are some things so ingrained they are beyond our ability to change? Should we just let these "sleeping dogs lie" and move on with our lives? Os IS it possible to CHANGE yourself?

☆ What does that experiment with the school children prove?

- If you believe you're smart, you act (and become) smart.

- If you believe you're creative, you act (and become) creative.

- If you believe you're a success, you act (and become) successful.

59

Dr. Jill Ammon-Wexler

- If you believe you're excellent, you act (and become) excellent.

Considering the results of this study, it's clear that your ability to transform yourself depends on what you BELIEVE. If you believe something is beyond your control, then it truly will be beyond your control. While if you BELIEVE you can change it, then you CAN.

What About Self Concept?

So let's cut straight to the point: If I ask you to describe yourself, what self-image will you paint? Another way to put this is, "Who do you *believe* you are?"

Your self concept is exactly what the word suggests - - *a collection of ideas* you have about yourself. It is how you view your personality, capabilities, skills, body, mind and personal potential. And while most people agree it is important to have a good self-image, few understand the big mystery about it.

The mystery? Your self concept is actually based on your reality at 5 years of age. This is not an exaggeration – it is solidly based on how our physical brains develop as we age.

The History of YOU

You first began to form your self concept and sense of personal worth as a very young child. You may have heard this before, but here's some insight into how this works:

The important people in your early childhood continually sent you messages about yourself. Why do the messages received from birth and up to about to age five or six have such a strong impact? This is so because of the way your physical brain develops.

You did not come into life with a fully developed adult brain. Your brain's emotional center (the limbic system) developed very young – so you DO feel and remember emotions from your earliest years. But your brain's memory creation and retrieval system is not fully developed until about age five or six, and sometimes even later.

As a result, from birth to 5 years you have a very open and impressionable mind that is tuned to

Dr. Jill Ammon-Wexler

emotional messages. But your brain's ability to actively recall these messages has NOT yet developed. That's why we seldom recall what happened to us before age five.

However the portion of your mind below consciousness – the subconscious mind – is fully operational at a very young age. Some believe it may even be active in the womb. The messages you received about yourself back then were stored in this portion of your mind. And the more intense the emotion attached to each of these old messages, the more powerful the impression it makes on your subconscious mind.

In a 1951 paper, Dr. Neal Miller wrote that although people can't remember their very early childhood, those events still influence them years later. "The young child does not notice or label the experiences it is having at this time," Miller wrote. "Nevertheless, the behavioral record survives."

Now, 50 years later, we finally know why this is so. The walnut-sized two amygdale and the hippocampus in your brain's limbic system are intimately involved in learning.

The amygdale apply the emotional meaning, and the hippocampus breaks the memory into pieces and stores it away for future reference.

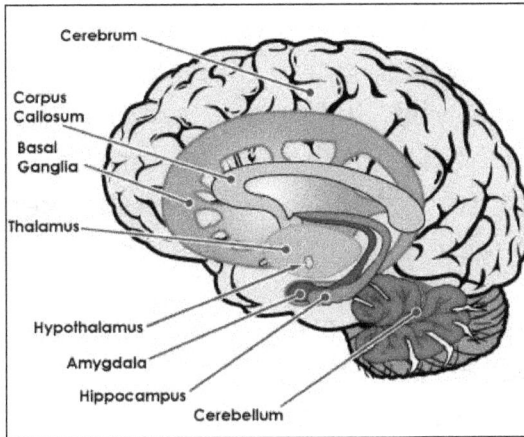

Recent research has proved the amygdale are present at birth – so your ability to attach an emotional meaning to something IS functional.

However the hippocampus only develops later on at about age 5 or 6. Therefore many events in our early childhood might leave an emotional memory imprint and influence our habits, but we might not have an actual conscious memory of these events due to our immature hippocampus.

Beliefs Then Form

These early emotion-packed subconscious memories are NOT normally available to our conscious mind. That puts them totally beyond "logical question," so they take on the power of *beliefs.*

63

Dr. Jill Ammon-Wexler

What happens next is this: Over the years other events are hooked onto these early subconscious beliefs. So if you have an early emotion-packed memory of being called a "dummy," any related events right up to today will be hooked onto the brain pathways holding that early "dummy" memory.

This is how our early subconscious beliefs grow into major personal limitations (or strengths) over the years! The result? As adults we tend to routinely believe we actually are our subconscious collection of other people's impressions of us as very young children.

⭐ Take a moment to grab this insight: There's a 100% probability your "personal limitations" do NOT even belong to you anymore. You have gone years beyond them, and it is only painful emotional memories stored in your subconscious mind that make those childhood judgments of you *seem* to still be true!

Are We Really What We Think?

The famous success teacher Earl Nightingale spent over 50 years of his life studying the world's philosophical, religious and metaphysical writings. Nightingale discovered a common thread among all of these writings: "We become what we think about."

Was he right? Do our thoughts really control who we become?

YES! It is now evident that "you become what you think about" is more than just an old saying. What you mentally FOCUS on actually creates your VERY REAL personal reality.

Here's how mental focus works in your physical brain: Picture a foot path through a meadow. Walking over the path every day creates a clear, well-defined path. But if you do not walk on the path, it will eventually grow over and disappear.

Your brain loves habit. Just like the path through that meadow, the cell-to-cell pathways in your brain are "worn in" (strengthened) by frequent use. And also like the path through the meadow, brain pathways tend to slowly weaken if left unused.

☆ Here's why we really ARE what we think: The more consciously (or subconsciously) you focus on a thought, the stronger the associated brain pathways become. This includes negative thoughts, which also grow when you focus on them.

If your center of attention is the bright side of life, on the other hand, your "positive" brain pathways will gain strength.

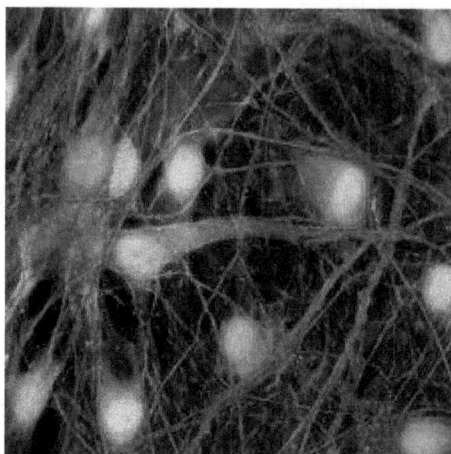

Artist's vision of a neural network

Does this seem too simple? It really IS that simple. This is not theory – it is proven scientific reality of how your brain works. What you focus on grows. Period!

Eliminate Limiting Thoughts

You were once just like those children in the Los Angeles classroom. Perhaps you remember something like the following story in your own life.

You're seven years old and want to learn to play baseball, but you have little experience catching, throwing or hitting the ball. One Saturday afternoon you grab your new birthday-present baseball mitt, and head down the block to watch the neighborhood kids play sandlot ball.

Finally you get up the courage to ask to join in. One of the older boys holds out his hand for your mitt, looks it over, nods his approval, and hands it back to you.

You're in, and you have been assigned to cover third base!

Your heart pounds as you take your place on the burlap bag marking third base. The pitcher throws a ball to first base, then one to second, and finally one to you. You clench your teeth and grab the ball out of the air. Your toss back to him is a little short, but you did manage to catch the ball and throw it back.

Then ten minutes into the inning there are now runners on first and second. The batter hits the pitch and it bounces across the ground right at you. You freeze as the ball bounces within inches of your foot. The pitcher and second baseman yell at you, but you're frozen in place on top of the third base burlap sack.

The second runner to pass third roughly pushes you off the burlap sack. All three runs score.

A chance to possibly redeem yourself comes with your turn to bat. You watched two other boys hit the ball, so you feel optimistic. You take your position at home plate with the bat on your shoulder. The first pitch slaps into the catcher's glove before you even begin to swing.

"Come on. Watch the ball," someone hollers.

You swing at the second pitch, but again you're too late. The third pitch is very slow. You glue your eyes onto the ball and start to swing. The pitch is so low it bounces off the plate, and your swing was knee high.

"You're out," the catcher shouts.

"You stupid dummy," a tall boy snarls at you when you hand him the bat. "Get out of here. Go play with the other babies."

After dinner you go to your father for support and advice. "I'm not surprised son," he says. "You're really not cut out for sports." That painful message physically tacks itself onto the raw memory of being thrown off the team and called a "dummy."

Now you have been hit with a double-whammy with the potential to cause some really serious self-esteem damage.

Are the ANTs Marching?

Are there some parts of your life where you frequently slam up against personal limitations? If so, you'll probably find a trail of bread crumbs leading right back into your early childhood. And a closer look will reveal a whole army of ANTs (**A**utomatic **N**egative **T**houghts) following along that trail.

What am I talking about?

ANTs are those nasty little negative thoughts that run through the back of your head when you're trying to do something new or challenging – those silent messages that insist you cannot do something, or you are in over your head, or you should quit rather than risk failure

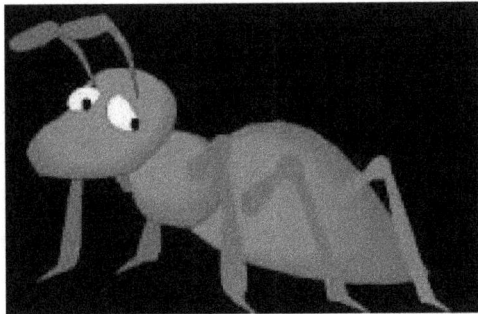

ANTs do not just go away by themselves. They are cemented in place by intense emotional content.

Any time you even think about doing something with an ANT attached to it, a whole army of ANTs will start to march through your brain. More times than not you will decide to "Just forget it" because "I'm

Dr. Jill Ammon-Wexler

not any good at that anyway." Or you'll agree to "try" something – fully expecting you're going to fail.

Sound familiar?

ANTs and Your Beliefs

We all have our own personal collection of ANTs. But they are not some bizarre enemy. Your ANTs are just trying to do what your brain thinks is best for you – protect you from pain. Where do ANTs come from? They're directly tied to limiting beliefs based on your 5-year-old self concept. And they now control what you can achieve TODAY!

So are you who you want to be? Are you living the life you want to live? If the answer is no, then it's time for an overhaul of your belief system. Anything else will just be a band-aid that will simply create more of the same.

Start by realizing that your beliefs do **NOT** reflect who you REALLY are today. You are far more than a collection of painful childhood memories. You are not that kid who was rudely told to speak only when spoken to. You are not that "clumsy" girl who only fell a lot because she needed glasses.

You are not "stupid" because you had more interest in drawing than reading and math. You are not "a failure" because your first lemonade stand (or MLM business) was a flop. You are none of those things.

In short: **You are <u>NOT</u> your past history.**

The experience of having more satisfaction and success in life begins with getting past your past. Stop automatically believing that old stuff, and stop acting as though it's true for who you are today and who you can become tomorrow!

Thoughts, Responses and Reality

Here's a summary of how you create your life:

- The thoughts you focus on determine how you respond to what happens to you, then

- How you *RESPOND* creates what you call your "personal reality."

⭐ You truly have created your personal reality with your thoughts, beliefs, and expectations. But the good news is this: Since you are the creative source, you also have the power to re-create your personal reality. How? By making conscious changes and adjustments in your personal beliefs and expectations.

Allowing your ANTs to have the upper hand creates what we call "personal limitations." This keeps you

71

Dr. Jill Ammon-Wexler

stuck in the worst experiences of your past, assuming that the present will be a repeat of the past and will create the same undesired outcomes.

This is NOT what you want!

Overhaul Your Beliefs

Here are some insights to help you polish up your reality-creating strategy:

ONE: Realize that you are NOT "ordinary." You are totally unique. There is literally no one else like you. No one else thinks like you, has your ideas, or does things the way you do. No one else has your unique set of talents and abilities. Your brain is as unique as your fingerprints. No one has your mind and memories. No one!

So stand up and carry yourself with dignity, because this IS your life. You and only you are living it, and it is your unique right to decide how to best do that. BE your original, unique self.

TWO: Learn to RESPOND – not just react. There is a huge difference between reacting and responding. Reacting is an automatic knee-jerk response to life. Responding involves making a conscious choice with your own best interests in mind.

We each truly create our own reality. You have a choice to simply REACT to what's happening to and around you, or you can choose to consciously RESPOND.

THREE: CHOOSE your own thoughts. Most of those old limiting beliefs about you will not hold up under conscious examination. Once you begin to challenge this old stuff, you'll find that your so-called "personal limits" do not really exist.

The greatest personal power you have is the power to CHOOSE your own thoughts. The late Earl Nightingale said, "You become what you think." The truth of this is so powerful it is almost overwhelming.

You and you alone decide what you will think, and what you believe your limits and potentials are. And you alone decide what to do with this awesome power.The fact is, you can recreate your self, and build and strengthen virtually any aspect of your life. Just CHOOSE to consciously build your own beliefs and take action.

FOUR: Begin to stamp out ANTs. To claim more of your true potential you will want to move those ant hills out of your subconscious mind. The following is a good ANT elimination method:

- **First**, identify the ANT you are after.

- **Second**, select a positive statement that is the exact opposite of what the ANT is saying. If you want to overcome fear of public speaking, for example, your new statement might be, "I am an excellent speaker." If you want to stomp out negative feelings about failure, you might say, "I am fearless and untouched by failure." Notice the term "I AM." Always use the present tense, because that's the message you want to cement into your brain connections.

- **Third**, do this exercise in private: Face a mirror and gaze straight into your own eyes. Once you're comfortable looking "into" yourself in this way, begin to repeat your statement while you continue to look right into your own eyes. Remember – emotion is important if you want to get your brain's attention.

Be sure to get as much emotional feeling into your statement as possible. Strong emotion will physically cement the new message into your brain. It does NOT matter if you believe your new positive statement at first. Repetition creates new brain connections for your new beliefs.

This is not theory – it is exactly how your brain really works. It's NOT that hard to install positive new beliefs to help yourself more easily move through life.

FIVE. HAVE A TOUGH CHILDHOOD?

When his father abandoned the family, this boy's mother faced the challenge of supporting a household on her own. But she totally lacked job skills and education.

"We just kept moving back and forth because my mother never had a steady job," he recalls. "We kept getting kicked out of every house we were in. I believe six months was the longest we ever lived in one house."

He was not a big kid, and was frequently bullied at school. At 8 years old he was so badly beaten by an older boy that he spent 10 days in a hospital very close to death. He turned to his uncle for moral support. But that too ended badly when his uncle died. He failed 9th grade three times, and finally gave up on continuing his formal education.

He recently wrote a song about his childhood experiences called "Brain Dead." Know who this is? The famous multi-millionaire rapper, Eminem!

Dr. Jill Ammon-Wexler

~~~~~~~~~~~~~~~~~

Many believe a tough childhood scars one forever. This does seem true for some. But this is not always the case.

His childhood was filled with constant terror of a violent drunken step-father. He survived years of unbelievable physical and emotional abuse, and became a very violent young man. But he took hold of himself and channeled his rage to become an Australian boxing champion.

When his childhood terror continued to haunt him he finally turned to writing to sort out his life. Today? He is now the creative director of one of the biggest advertising agencies in the world. His name? Shane Weaver, also the successful author of "Blacktown."

~~~~~~~~~~~~~~~~~

She quit school to marry at 17 and promptly had three children one after the other. When her husband went off to fight WWII, she grabbed the only job she could get selling books door-to-door. But this young mother amazed everyone, earning an outrageous $25,000 in just six months.

When her husband returned from the war they ended up divorcing. Then in spite of her lack of a college education and no business experience, she fought her way tooth-and-nail to become a top sales director in a home products company.

But in 1963, after 25 years of being refused the promotions and pay raises going to men, she quit. She then took her life savings of $5,000 and opened a small store in Dallas. Who was this woman? The late Mary Kay Ash – the gutsy founder of today's huge worldwide personal care business "Mary Kay."

Advantages of a Tough Childhood

We all have obstacles and hardships – some of us far more than others. The old belief is that if you had a tough childhood, you will likely continue to have problems over your entire lifetime and have far less probability of success.

Many psychologists do feel that childhood trauma "damages" a person and makes their success and happiness far less likely. There is no doubt that a difficult childhood leaves some people deeply wounded and disadvantaged.

But DOES a tough childhood necessarily make success less probable?Actually the opposite seems true. There's a lot of evidence that intense difficulties, hardships and obstacles are often MAJOR contributors to a person's success. And for some, their tough childhood seems to drive them to even more outrageous achievement and success.

What makes these people so different? Let's take a closer look at the evidence:

In a classic book entitled "*Cradles of Eminence*," co-authors Victor and Mildred Goertzel reviewed the childhood family life of 700 of the world's most successful people. Their goal was to identify the early experiences that contributed to their remarkable achievements.

All of their research subjects are quite well known and their names easily recognizable: Franklin D. Roosevelt, Helen Keller, Winston Churchill, Albert Schweitzer, Gandhi, Albert Einstein, Sigmund Freud, etc.

What they discovered is fascinating. The majority of these successful people (525 of the 700) came from deeply troubled childhoods. They endured extreme poverty, broken homes, and even serious physical and emotional parental abuse.

One out of every four (199 of the 700) had serious physical handicaps such as deafness, disfigurations, blindness or crippled limbs. And in the case of the successful writers and playwrights in the group, over

80% watched their parents struggle through some very intense and painful psychological dramas.The Goertzel's concluded that their drive to compensate for disadvantages drove these people straight into the arms of outrageous personal achievement. A remarkable conclusion!

Triumph of a "Homely" Woman

What follows is another amazing true story:

Anna had a childhood of utter anguish. She was orphaned at age 10, and was painfully aware of being very homely. Her childhood writings reveal that she never had a sense of "belonging" anywhere, or to anyone.

As a child she was described by a writer of her time as being "a rather humorless introvert, unbelievably shy, unable to overcome her personal insecurity, and with a deep conviction of her own inadequacies."

But this unattractive young woman refused to remain "disadvantaged." She took hold of her own bootstraps and began to pull herself up into a higher, more powerful consciousness.

After marrying, she courageously nursed her husband through crippling polio. Then when he (Franklin Roosevelt) was elected to the U.S.

Presidency in the depth of the Great Depression, she immediately transformed the position of First Lady.

So do you consider yourself "too busy" to reach out and claim your full potential? As the First Lady, this deeply compassionate woman became an outspoken supporter for the downtrodden of all races, religions and countries – at the same time managing the White House and raising six children.

The Amazing Eleanor Roosevelt

After her husband's death she spent the remainder of her life as a highly-respected spokesperson to the United Nations. At her death this formerly shy, disadvantaged, homely and withdrawn woman had become one of the most loved and revered women of her entire generation.

How and why did this happen? It happened because she made a *Personal Choice* to lift herself beyond her perceived "limitations." As writer Victor Wilson said, "From some inner wellspring, Eleanor Roosevelt summoned a tough, unyielding courage, tempered by remarkable self-control and self-discipline."

Anna Eleanor Roosevelt provides an excellent example of how adversity can lead YOU to your own outrageous greatness.

Have a Tough Childhood?

Modern science has provided proof that "well-being" is NOT necessarily an advantage to either plants or animals. Where there is no challenge, obstacle or hardship – growth and development are often limited. Biologists refer to this as the "adversity principle."

You have the same transformational potential as Eleanor Roosevelt, Eminem, Mary Kay Ash and all other self-made winners. Obstacles and hardships do *not* have to lead to failure.

Adversity causes some people to break, and others to break records. It's a personal choice! Consider these real-life examples:

Lou was such a clumsy kid that the boys in his neighborhood wouldn't let him play sandlot baseball with them. But Lou Gehrig tapped into his own inner source of courage and determination. He's today listed in the "Baseball Hall of Fame" as one of the greatest ball players of all time.

Woodrow Wilson could not read until he was ten years old, yet went on to become the twenty-eighth President of the United States. The great inventor Thomas Edison was stone-cold deaf. The famed speaker and activist Booker T. Washington was born into slavery.

As a young child the brilliant Albert Einstein was considered a hopeless dyslexic who could not be educated. Alexander Pope had an unsightly hunchback. Julius Caesar was an epileptic.

Yet each of these individuals became famous historic figures in spite of, or perhaps because of, their serious handicaps.

And how about Helen Keller who could not hear or see, yet shocked an entire nation when she graduated from college with honors.

Then there's Ludwig Beethoven, who began to lose his hearing in his 20s and was completely deaf by 50. Yet he created some of the world's most beautiful music. He was once overheard shouting at the top of his voice, "I will take life by the throat!"

STOP Being "Realistic"

Most of us were taught that having a "realistic" opinion of ourselves is basic to sound mental health and happiness. But is this really true? Could we do better to indulge in "self-illusions?"

It's commonly assumed that normal, well-adjusted people have realistic views of their own potential. And it is also commonly assumed that those who do not have realistic self-concepts are very possibly neurotic or unbalanced.

So are these assumptions true? I'll have to say absolutely NOT. As a psychologist for over 45 years, the healthiest and happiest people I've known are totally unrealistic about themselves. In short – they have what some might call "unrealistically optimistic illusions" about their own capabilities and potential.

So could this actually be a good thing? Let's take a look at some recent research and clinical evidence.

A short self-evaluation test was used to divide a group of college freshmen into two groups: Those who were "extremely optimistic" about their probable success, and those who said they are "more realistic" about their chances for success.

The research team then gave a series of psychological tests to each group. The "extremely optimistic" students tended to:

- Exaggerate their positive qualities,

- See themselves as more ethical, creative, imaginative and intelligent than they really were, and

- Dismiss their personal flaws as unimportant.

Does that sound "healthy?" Yet the personal interviews of the optimistic group showed them to be very well-adjusted, happy, and not focused on any negative aspects of their own personality.

So what about those who were more "realistic" about themselves? This may come as quite a surprise. Their personal interviews revealed that many of them suffered from depression and negativity, and they were far were less likely to achieve their goals.

I have personally found that having "unrealistically high optimism" about your self also tends to increase your motivation and persistence. It therefore increases the probability you will achieve your goals. This obviously leads to a more satisfying life experience.

If you tend to be "realistic" about your own "limitations," you might want to take a few minutes to think about this.

Your *attitude* toward any personal "handicap" you believe you have determines its impact on your life. That's it! Your *attitude*. And your attitude is entirely under YOUR control. Remember this, the next time you're tempted to focus on any personal "weaknesses" or past pain to justify a "failure."

If you feel sick and tired of settling for less in your life, this is a good day to take action and claim more of your true potential. To move past any old "negative stuff," and fire yourself up. If not now, when?

Here are some tips to help you get started on this right now, today:

Got Excuses? To become all you can be, you will want to stop making excuses. Use any personal adversity or perceived limitation to do what Beethoven did – let lose with a life-affirming roar and just "grab life by the throat."

Use Self Talk. Self-talk is a very powerful tool. Pick one of your less-desirable personal beliefs. Start to challenge it using self-talk. "I'll never make a friend"

85

Dr. Jill Ammon-Wexler

becomes, "I'm a friendly person, and can make new friends easily."

This is not some "Pollyanna" approach – it's actually a powerful, proven-effective mental reprogramming method. What you're doing is creating some very real *new* physical brain cell-to-cell pathways in your brain.

Learn the Duchenne Smile. Scientists have pinpointed the exact spot in your brain that controls your ability to "think positive." It is a small portion of your left cerebral cortex. Some people seem to have a natural activation of this part of their brain. And interestingly, they tend to be naturally positive and optimistic.

Others have very low energy in this part of their brain, and tend to be self-judging, negative, and depressed. Many of these folks were labeled shy or withdrawn as children – so there is evidence this starts very early in life.

If you're a "realist" who would rather be an optimist, you will want to learn to turn on this portion of your left frontal lobe – the side responsible for those great "unrealistic" feelings about your own potential.

Brain scans have shown that laughter is a strong activator of this part of the brain, and so is a genuine smile.

The type of smile you are after is called the "Duchenne smile," after a 19th century French researcher, Guillaume Duchenne. Duchenne is credited with discovering the difference between a "social smile" and the type of genuine smile now known to light up the "happiness center" in your left cortex.

Polite social smiles do *not* activate the same portions of your face, or your brain. Go look at yourself in the mirror and watch the muscles around your eyes as you smile.

George Clooney's Duchenne smile

A Duchenne smile makes crinkles around your eyes. Smile until your facial skin gathers inward toward your eye sockets. Take a look at George Clooney's picture. Notice how his cheeks are raised and he had "crinkles" around his eyes. This is a genuine Duchenne smile.

Dr. Jill Ammon-Wexler

Duchenne smiles activate the portion of your brain associated with happy, optimistic feelings. Each time you turn on this portion of your brain, you pump up your brain's ability to create positive, optimistic thoughts. It really is that simple and gives you the kind of smile that lights up your face.

And here's an interesting bit of research info: Researchers found that when talking on the telephone, a stranger on the other end can tell if you are smiling a "social" smile or a genuine (Duchenne) smile. So there's a tip if you happen to do business on the telephone!

Put it Into Words. Picture yourself in a UCLA psychology laboratory. Your brain is being monitored as you play a computer game called Cyberball. You're enjoying playing "catch" on-screen with two other people.

For a while the two others throw the ball regularly to your on-screen character. You're getting pretty good at it – then suddenly the other two players throw the ball only to each other, cutting you out of the game.

You feel the pain of social rejection. This turns on an area of your brain that also lights up when you feel physical pain (the *anterior cingulate cortex*). But interestingly, when you then speak of your distress to the researcher, the part of your brain tied to emotional distress then turns *OFF.*

The psychologist behind of this research, Dr. Matthew Lieberman, laughingly told a convention of thousands of psychologists, "Tell your troubles to a Guatemalan worry doll, place it beneath your pillow and, according to legend, those worries will be gone by morning."

The worry doll aside, Lieberman's research did provide proof that *just* putting your problems into words can actually ease your emotional pain.

Stomp Your ANTs. ANTs (Automatic Negative Thoughts) can undo your most determined efforts to create a healthy, happy, successful, prosperous life. They are the enemy of anyone desiring lasting personal change.

☆ **Here are four steps to <u>stomp</u> some of your ANTs:**

First, build your awareness of what your ANTs are all about. What messages are they marching through the back of your mind? Do NOT just "stuff" them back down for another day.

Pay attention to the songs that float through the back of your mind, and try to identify the words to the song. You may be very surprised at the "theme songs" your subconscious mind is using to conceal ANTs – or to try to lift you up.

Second, once you become aware of an ANT, drag it out into the sunlight of your conscious mind. Ask yourself if the ANT providing a message about something you should change? Or is it just spouting "old stuff" from age five that's no longer really true for you?

Third, create an "anchor" to signal to yourself that you are stomping an ANT. An anchor is a signal to yourself that will become automatic once established. For example, you could snap your fingers every time you beat down an ANT that tries to undo your efforts to improve your life. Come up with your own personal anchors.

Fourth, remember that your brain can really only consciously focus on *one* thought at a time. Focus your conscious thoughts on what you want. Do NOT permit yourself to focus on worry or limitation. Worry is actually negative goal setting. Remember: What you focus on will grow.

SIX. THE POWER OF BELIEF

Here's another amazing true story: A young man believes he is dead – literally a walking corpse. His exasperated parents finally take him to a highly respected New York City psychiatrist.

The young man and the psychiatrist argue the reality of his "walking death reality" back and forth.

The psychiatrist tries to convince the young man he's not a walking corpse, and that he is certainly not dead. The young man argues back and will not yield his belief he is dead. Finally the psychiatrist gets an idea he's certain will convince the young man that his odd belief is incorrect. He asks the young man, "Do you believe that dead people bleed?"

The young man thinks about this for a moment, then shakes his head, "No, all the body functions stop when you're dead. So there will be no blood flowing."

The psychiatrist then walks to his desk and pulls a needle from a small button-sewing kit. He casually crosses the room. "Let me see your right hand," he

91

says. The young man holds out his hand. The psychiatrist suddenly pricks the young man's index with the needle.

The young man gasps and stares at his finger in amazement. "Well," he finally stammers. "I'll be darned. Dead people DO bleed!"

Beliefs <u>Create</u> Your Reality

Have you ever challenged someone's political or religious beliefs with a logic-based question? If you did, then you surely noticed how emotional and defensive they became. Our beliefs about our own self share the same attribute – they resist logical challenge, and are closely tied to our emotional brain.

Something far beyond logic and reason truly DOES create and sustain our beliefs. What is it? Think about that young man who was totally convince he was a "walking corpse." His belief was so powerful that logical evidence had no influence at all.

What does that say about our beliefs?

We all tend to just believe that our beliefs are absolutely true – even in the face of undeniable evidence they *not* true. This is especially true of our beliefs about our own self. And note that such beliefs are <u>NOT</u> necessarily tied to any logical reality at all!

Why is this so?

Suppose as a young child you were called "clumsy," and you came to believe that was true. I'll bet if I gave you a motor skills test <u>proving</u> that you actually have above-average coordination, you would "poo poo" the test as meaningless. Why? Because your belief that you're clumsy will just run right over any external evidence.

So ... in terms of learning to soar through life more easily, examining your beliefs is a good place to start. Do you believe you lack self-confidence, are a poor public speaker, will never be successful, or perhaps cannot create a good relationship?

Then guess what? You will defend that belief, even to yourself. That's just built into the powerful nature of our "beliefs." Let's proceed...

The Emotional Connection

Beliefs are far more connected to emotion then to logic. They come pre-packaged with intense emotion because they are actually created in your emotional brain. And the intense emotion of beliefs tends to hold them in place in your brain like "cement."

Dr. Jill Ammon-Wexler

This makes your brain automatically resist any attempt to question a belief with reason or logic. Ifyou believe something to be true, your subconscious mind will then *automatically* filter everything you see, feel and do through that belief. In short, your beliefs actually DO define and create your "personal reality."

As you now know, strong emotions create powerful brain connections. And our beliefs are held together with tough emotional cement. That's why they have such a powerful hold over us. And that is also why we often get intensely emotional if someone dares to question one of our beliefs.

We truly do believe that our beliefs are true. You do not have to stop and think about it when you "believe" something. You just believe it. Period!

And here is an interesting point: Since we assume our beliefs about our self are also beyond logical question, they often go unquestioned even by our own self. That leaves us believing, and often defending, something that may not even be true for who we are today!

The Power of a Positive Belief

Thanksgiving evening, 1987: A 25-year-old stand-up comic pulls his aged Toyota Corolla into a vista point high in the Hollywood Hills. He turns off the radio and sits quietly by himself watching the lights come on down in the valley, thinking of his future. Suddenly he pulls out his checkbook, writes himself a check for $10 million dated for Thanksgiving Day, 1995, and carefully inserts the check into his wallet.

But the hopeful projection of this young man proved to be way off. His roles in "Ace Ventura: Pet Detective," "The Mask," and "Dumb & Dumber" produced returns of $550 million. By the date of his $10 million check, Jim Carrey's acting price had soared to $20 million a movie.

Here's another example of how visualization can strengthen a positive belief, and that belief then creates reality:

The great golfing legend Jack Nicklaus says, "I never hit a shot, not even in practice, without having a very sharp, in-focus picture of it in my head. First," he says, "I see the ball where I want it to finish – nice and white, sitting up high on the bright green grass. Then the scene quickly changes, and I see the ball going there; its path, trajectory, and shape, even its behavior on landing. Then there is a sort of fade-out … and the next scene shows me making the kind of swing that will turn the previous images into reality."

Dr. Jill Ammon-Wexler

Beliefs are Like Superglue

⭐ Your beliefs about your strengths and your limitations are the superglue that truly determines who you are, and what you will accomplish in your lifetime.

Henry Ford, the visionary inventor of the modern automobile, said, "Whether you believe you can or believe you can't, you're absolutely right.

We each have a set of beliefs for every area of our life – from money and success, to relationships and body image. And as you now realize, most of your beliefs date straight back to your first five years of life. A great way to raise your "success probability" without struggle or by trying harder is to just look closely at what you today believe about yourself.

What I am about to share with you truly shocked me when I first learned it from Deepak Chopra in his book, *"Life After Death: The Burden of Proof."* It seems our power of belief not only creates the reality of our current life – it also carries over into our near-death experiences.

After studying the experiences of people from many different cultures and belief systems, Chopra discovered an interesting phenomenon: Those with a Buddhist belief system experience a "Buddhist reality" during a near-death experience. While those who believe they'll be met by someone they love on the other side experience just that.

What does this say about the power of belief to create your reality?

Another True Story

Once you have identified a limiting belief, then you're in a position to do something about it! I discovered years ago how a single thought can overturn even the most engrained belief. Here's a real life example of the power of changing a belief:

The wife of a prominent local surgeon came into my clinic one day looking for relief from crippling back pain. She wanted to avoid surgery if possible.

Mrs. Joanne Robbins (not her real name) had been in a car crash almost three years earlier and had wrenched her back. Her back pain had never healed, and she shuffled into the office leaning heavily on a cane, although she was only 38 years old.

In the first session Joanne expressed the belief she would never heal. She explained through racking tears that she had been driving and her best friend had died in the crash. She said she would never forgive herself.

I attached biofeedback sensors to her back and we both watched the computer EMG readings go wild as she painfully tried to move her legs. I then attached biofeedback sensors to her right arm, and had her tense and relax her arm muscles. She watched the screen, agreeing that the screen images for "relaxed" and "tense" were very different.

Then I suggested to Joanne that her back pain might be due to muscle bracing that had become a chronic habit, and proposed an experiment in which she would just "think" about allowing her back to relax.

I again placed feedback sensors on her back and turned the screen away from her as she began to just 'think about' relaxing her back muscles. The pain spikes on the biofeedback screen dropped dramatically. I froze the screen and rotated it for her to view.

She was amazed to see how only a thought had immediately affected the chronic muscle spasms in her back. I asked her how her back felt. She noticed her skin felt warmer, as her circulation had been partially restored as the spasms relaxed.

After only three biofeedback sessions Joanne had learned to release the muscle spasms in her back with a single thought. A few weeks later the cane was gone. She had cured herself from a crippling belief ("I don't think I'll ever heal") with a single powerful alternative belief ("I can relax the muscle spasms in my back at will.") Emotional healing around the loss of her friend soon followed.

Old beliefs absolutely can be replaced with success-affirming positive new beliefs.

Beliefs Actually <u>CHANGE</u> Reality

For many years it was universally believed that no one would ever run a mile in four minutes. The athletes of the time held this belief, and the scientific and coaching world totally agreed.

But there was one man who did not agree. In fact this man firmly believed this barrier could be broken, and that he would be the one to do so. The name of this remarkable rebel was Roger Bannister.

On May 6, 1954 Roger Bannister did indeed run the first historically-recorded "4-minute mile." But even more interesting, just six weeks later Australian runner John Lundy cut a second off Bannister's record. And in the following ten years almost two hundred people also broke this so-called "impossible" barrier.

Why did this happen? Because Bannister shattered the *belief* that this was impossible. And when the belief fell, the 4-minute mile suddenly became an achievable reality. Is that amazing?

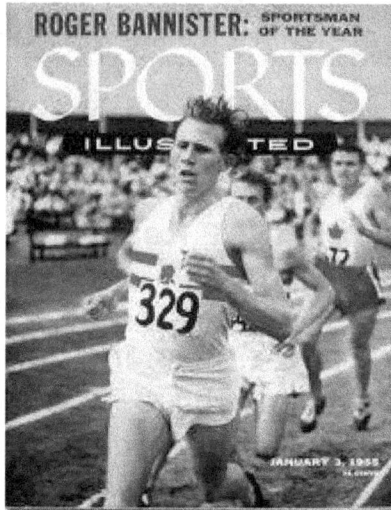

The impossible 4-minute mile
proves possible!

Challenge Your Limiting Beliefs

Your collection of personal beliefs literally draws the line around what you can (and cannot) achieve in your life.

If your beliefs about yourself and your potential are positive and empowering, your world is full of opportunities and success. But if you have negative limiting beliefs about yourself and your potential, your life will be filled with one disappointment, frustration and failure after another. That's just the way beliefs work. And interestingly, other people reflect our beliefs right back to us!

Do you wish to get what you want in life a lot easier? Go after the old limiting beliefs holding you back. This begins with having the personal courage to identify them. Once you identify a belief that's somehow limiting you, it's time to go to work.

☆ Start by reminding yourself that your beliefs are only *habitual ways of thinking*. Like any habit, your beliefs CAN be revised.

Beliefs are habits, and the best way to change a habit is to replace it with a new habit. Here's how that works with old limiting beliefs: Begin to jump on an ANT the very moment it enters your consciousness. Identify what current reality triggered it so you will know what it is tied to. Then take immediate action to replace it with an emotion-charged positive new statement.

Your brain is a creature of habit. The more often you consciously focus on a new belief, the faster your subconscious mind will accept it as true. What you are doing is starving the brain network dedicated to th old limiting habit, and replacing it with a new physical brain network holding a positive, emotion-charged belief.

101

Remember – this happens on an actual *physical* level in your brain. The power of a positive emotionally charged message is amazing. You are changing your brain on a cellular level, and modern science has the tools to actually watch this happen.

Following are some strategies that will help move you forward:

Change Your Destiny. I'm sure you know what your "genetic inheritance" is – the genetic code you inherited from your parents. But here's a question: Do you believe you are somehow limited by your genetic inheritance?

Yes? That's not surprising, since that's what we were all taught in school. But there is one brilliant scientist and medical school professor that wants to change your mind about the so-called power of your genes.

Doctor Bruce H. Lipton radically disagrees with the old belief that our physical and mental capabilities are "pre-programmed" by our genes. He is a renowned leader in cell science, and represents a new movement in cell biology.

He and other leading cell biologists now say that our personal *interpretation* of what's happening around us directly controls the actual activity of our genes.

☆ Consider the implication of this: Our genes do *NOT* control who and what we are, nor do they control our potentials. Each of us controls the "expression" of our genes. Lipton explains that although every one of your cells is a free-living entity, the combined "cellular community" of your body responds to the orders of ONE central voice – your mind.

This is just another example of the amazing power of your brain, and how you use it to create your personal reality.

Create New Mental Pictures. Virtually ANY lasting improvement in your life will always start with an improvement in your mental pictures. Mental pictures are a powerful life guidance mechanism. They sit in your brain and formulate and strengthen the beliefs and actions that allow you to create what you wish to be and do in your life.

Top achievers always "envision their future" inside their minds before they manifest it on the outside.

Pay Attention to ANTs. Overhauling a limiting belief requires some detective work. Here is where to start: If you have a limiting belief about your own potential, you will notice you also have ANTs constantly reminding you of that belief. And since

Dr. Jill Ammon-Wexler

ANTs come out of your subconscious mind they will often also appear in your dreams and daydreams.

If you want to override a limiting personal belief, the best place to start is with your ANTs. Begin to pay attention to what those ANTs are saying to you.

Track them back into your childhood by asking yourself who said that about you as a child? What were the circumstances? Then stand back and ask yourself is this necessarily true today? What is the evidence?

What you are looking for is a glimpse of the *real* truth beyond your old beliefs about yourself.

As you drag ANTs out into the daylight of your conscious mind, you'll often find they may have been true for you as a child, but are not true for you as an adult. Today, as an adult, you have the power to make a conscious change.

This is important. You don't want to set your sights on a new vision – just to be shot down by some ANT tied to an outdated personal belief system!

Use the Power of One Minute

Want to get started making some amazing positive gains in your life? Then how about doing a one-minute mini life improver right now? The biggest goal is accomplished only one step at a time. And a new belief is created one thought at a time. Each positive minute adds to your belief you can make your life a better, more successful place to be.

Here are some great ways to use the amazing power of one minute:

- **Exercise for one minute.** No time to go to the gym? OK. Forget about the next 59 minutes and just focus on the next minute. Do a deep breathing exercise, or one minute of push-ups or sit-ups. After a while you may expand to two minutes – and you've made a 200% jump.

- **Relax for one minute**. Just relax into your chair and suck in a slow deep breath all the way down into your belly. Then open your mouth slightly, and release your breath as slowly as you can. Try this right now to refresh your mind with increased oxygen.

- **Calm your mind for one minute**. Your mind is a fabulous theater and contains wonderful visions of your favorite places. Go visit one of those places for one minute. Just relax and clear your mind wherever you may be. You'll come away feeling refreshed, and a lot calmer and clearer.

105

- **Change your outlook for one minute.** You can even experiment going outside your normal self for a minute. Try acting the exact opposite of how you usually act for one minute. If you tend to be introverted, think like an extrovert. If you are an engineer, think like an artist. If you're a man, try thinking like a woman for one minute

- **Re-frame a problem for one minute.** Choose a problem, and then select a different "frame of reference" to consider it from. Try considering the problem through the eyes of someone you admire.

- Does the problem look different? Try looking at it with the mind Albert Einstein or Bill Gates or Oprah. Now how does the problem look?

- **Be happy for one minute.** Do you feel overwhelmed with problems and challenges beyond your control? If so, try finding something to give thanks for and spend one minute focusing on being grateful.

Forget any current or past tragedies or disasters, and just let yourself be happy for one minute. You really can achieve wonders in just one minute. And these single minutes can add up to a greatly improved quality of life. Pick one right now and make a positive investment in yourself.

Dr. Jill Ammon-Wexler

SEVEN. THE POWER OF OPTIMISM

You meet one of your friends, Marie, for coffee. But she's clearly not herself. She keeps staring down at the table. You reach across the table and tap her on the arm. "Hello? Anyone home?" you ask playfully.

Marie looks up, and you can see she's obviously choking back tears.

"What's wrong?" you ask. You can see she's very upset, so you slide a $5 bill under your cup to pay for the coffee and suggest a walk.

You settle onto a park bench and Marie finally reveals what's eating at her. She's been worried for some time about her business, a small gift shop just off Market Street. Business has reached an all time low, and she's thinking of closing it down.

"I knew this was going to happen months ago," she sighs. "I knew it even before I went to the gift show to buy my current inventory. I think I've always known it."

As she continues you start to get the whole picture. Your friend was afraid from the very first day she opened her shop two years ago. Her aunt once had a gift shop that failed in the second year, and she lost everything.

Your friend Marie has spent the past two years worrying about failing just like her aunt. And now her worries seem to be coming true.

☆ What is worry? Worry is commonly assumed to be a natural part of life. But stop and think about that for a moment. Worry only occurs when you're focused on the future and are afraid that something negative *could* happen. Is it acceptable to focus on something negative that isn't even happening, and might never happen?

Why Worries "Come True"

Remember that old saying, "Be careful what you think about, because it will probably come true." It's interesting how these old sayings contain so much wisdom. Let's take a look at what is behind this one.

Worry *begins* as a CHOICE, and can then quickly become a habitual mental pattern. So here's a new definition of worry for you to think about: *Worry is actually negative goal setting.* And that is why worries tend to "come true."

Picture each of your thoughts as a mental photograph. When a new thought is first exposed to your brain very little happens. But as you expose your brain again and again to that thought, it starts to develop as a lasting image in your mind's eye – just like the film in a camera holds images that can be developed into lasting photographs.

⭐ In fact, your thoughts really are that powerful. Anything you focus on mentally does develop such "images" in the form of well-established physical networks connecting your brain cells to other brain cells.

Our persistent thoughts then direct our actions. This is not theory. It's based on the research findings of modern neuroscience. We truly are the very powerful creators of our own reality –whether positive or negative.

111

Dr. Jill Ammon-Wexler

Negative Goal Setting

Because of the power of repeated thoughts, you want to be careful about your worries, judgments, beliefs and opinions.

If you focus your mind on something you do not want, you will strengthen the physical connections of the brain cells containing the image of that very thing. That's why worrying about something drives you closer to what you are worried about.

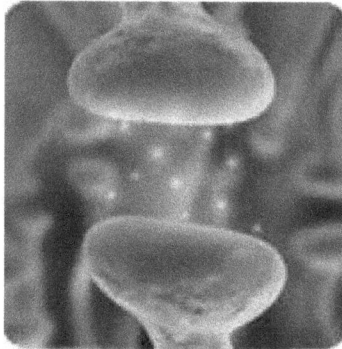

Artist's depiction of a
neurotransmitter site

Worrying IS powerful negative goal setting! The more you worry about something, the stronger the brain's neurotransmiter pathways containing that worry will become.

This makes it more likely your subconscious mind will drive you to take actions pushing you toward exactly what you're worried about.

Does Positive Thinking Help?

Have you ever tried to "think positive" as a way to overcome your worries? Then you've already discovered that by itself, just thinking positive usually does NOT get you what you want. There's a reason for this.

If just thinking a thought would automatically create what we are thinking of, then everyone that has read Napoleon Hill's book *Think and Grow Rich* would today be rich. Obviously there's something happening behind the scenes. This something is about being positive and taking positive ACTION – NOT just thinking about it.

That's why it's entirely possible to think positive, but still have a mind packed with crippling worries. But there's an answer.

Power of "Intelligent Optimism"

What can you do when you slam up against a brick wall? When your brain feels is clogged with worry? When you're thinking about making a change, but feel blocked or discouraged?

☆ We all slam up against brick walls on occasion. Life can be tough, but one thing is always true: We each have a CHOICE of how to *interpret* what's happening, and also how we CHOOSE to respond. The best way to break free of the worry habit is to CHOOSE to learn optimism.

By optimism I am NOT referring to some Pollyanna "everything is wonderful" attitude. And I'm NOT referring to simple "positive thinking." True optimism goes far beyond the concept of positive thinking. I'm referring to a refined mental style of how you CHOOSE to respond to life.

The dictionary defines optimism as, "A tendency to put the most favorable interpretation on actions and events, or to expect the best possible outcome."

The type of optimism I'm referring to does NOT deny reality. It's NOT being idealistic or chasing after some unrealistic condition or situation. The optimism I'm referring is focused on an attitude that does not deny problems, but rather adjusts to them, while actively seeking an opportunity for progress.

There is basically only one thing optimism and pessimism have in common – they are both self-fulfilling. So if you are optimistic, good things will happen in your life. And if you are pessimistic, less desirable things will occur in your life. Our attitudes toward life shape our entire reality.

Optimists tend to be basically happy people, even in the face of huge personal challenges. But have you ever known a happy pessimist?

How do you recognize an optimist? An optimist is a person who has a personal belief that what happened in their past was basically good for them, even if it was painful. They also believe that everything in the present is somehow manageable, and that the future will be even better.

The specific attitudes that characterize an intelligent optimist include:

- They don't let themselves get carried away by circumstances they cannot change, and instead focus on things they can control or influence.

- They know that for every problem there is at least the beginning of a solution, and that the search for that solution can be fulfilling in itself.

- They persevere and persist in the face of setbacks.

- They look for insight that will fire them up, and tend to focus on positive thoughts that encourage, energize, and lead to action.

Dr. Jill Ammon-Wexler

- They are not afraid of ANTs, which they realize are just internal messages they can choose to listen to, change, or even reject.

Your Brain's Optimism Center

Remember the earlier mention of your brain's "optimism center" – the part of your left prefrontal cortex that makes the brain-level difference between optimists and pessimists? Well those who tell you to "just think positive" are missing a key point. Unless you know how to activate this part of your brain, you will never be able to think and act positive.

One prominent neuroscientist, Dr. Richard J. Davidson, is especially interested in how people vary in this part of the brain. "Some people walk around on a daily basis with the left prefrontal region more activated," he tells us. "Others walk around with their right prefrontal regions more activated. The differences are consistent over time, and correspond with certain personality traits, attitudes, and emotions."

People with a more active left prefrontal cortex are more cheerful, enthusiastic, alert, and actively engaged in life. They are also more persistent when pursuing a goal, and recovery rapidly from negative events. They are, in short, natural intelligent optimists.

116

On the other hand, people with natural activation of the right prefrontal cortex are natural pessimists. They have trouble turning off negative emotions, tend to hold on to memories of negative life events, and take longer to recover from painful experiences.

Learn Intelligent Optimism

There's strong scientific evidence we can LEARN to voluntarily turn on the "optimism center" in our left prefrontal cortex. One very interesting research project studied a group of people who were "tipped toward the right" and tended to complain about feeling stressed and unhappy at work.

The entire group was trained in a form of meditation called "mindfulness training." During the training the participants' emotions became more positive and their moods improved. Brain scans showed more activation in their left prefrontal cortex (the positive emotion side).

The research team concluded that with proper training, one's brain-based "emotional set points" *can* be shifted from negative to positive.

In short – if you are not a natural optimist, you can *become* one. In addition to mindfulness training, equally effective ways to activate this brain center include engineered brainwave training, laughter, and the special type of real Duchenne smile I mentioned earlier – smile until you get "crinkle lines" around your eyes.

Studies show that optimism leads to more success in school, and a fatter paycheck after school. In a study of law students, researchers found that the level of optimism in the first year of law school corresponded to actual salary 10 years later. The impact was substantial. On a scale from 1 to 5, every 1-point increase in optimism translated into a $33,000 increase in eventual annual income.

Did you know that you can actually "trick" your brain into making you feel happy and optimistic? Dr. David Lykken, a professor at the University of Minnesota says, "Emotions are a combination of internal feelings and physical responses that provide feedback to your brain."

Try the following strategies to create a more positive, optimistic outlook:

- **Smile** even when you don't feel like it. Many studies have shown that people who force themselves to smile eventually DO develop a more positive attitude. Smile the moment you wake up.

Smile as you put yourself to sleep. Smile at everyone you meet. But make sure it's a real Duchenne smile – the one proven to light up the "positive outlook" center in your left prefrontal cortex.

- **Laugh.** Get some air into your lungs. More oxygen equals more energy and a brighter day. In Japan many companies now have their employees take a daily "laughter break." The employees gather outside, form a circle, and force themselves to laugh non-stop for 15 minutes. Company executives swear this laughter break causes worker enthusiasm and productivity to soar.

- **Stand Tall.** Remember your teacher or parent insisting, "No slouching! Chin up! Walk tall!" They were not just pushing you to develop good posture. They were also helping you develop an optimistic and confident outlook in life. Your body and brain are intimately connected. A confident posture communicates confidence to your brain.

Get Back to Basics

When you're looking to increase your personal power, a good strategy is to just get back to basics.

Dr. Jill Ammon-Wexler

Take a good, honest look at where you are, what you're doing, and what you're not doing.

Examine everything. Where are you spending your time and money? Are you receiving the value you really want from those expenditures? Does what you're spending money and time on match your basic core values? Demand honest answers from yourself.

Here are some questions to get you started:

Q. What are the most important things in my life?

Q. How much of my time is focused on these things?

Q. What do I really want?

Q. Why do I want it?

Q. Am I ready to go after it?

Q. How can I create time to focus on what I truly want?

Q. Am I taking actions that support my answers to these questions?

Focus on Solutions

When you catch yourself thinking or saying something negative, just stop. Change your sentences into positives. Since what you focus on grows, it is obviously important NOT to focus on your problems! A far better solution is to focus on positive solutions that will create something you do want. Pessimists focus and complain of problems. Optimists focus on finding solutions.

Here's how to get started:

- Convert your problems to positive, achievable goals,

- Think through and create a realistic detailed goal-plan,

- Break your goal-plan into the smallest possible daily steps, then

- Begin TODAY to take daily action – one step at a time.

Dr. Jill Ammon-Wexler

EIGHT. ACTIVATE YOUR GENIUS

My dear Mother, rest her brilliant and creative soul, convinced me early on that I was destined for a creative life.

Although I came from a very hard working family, certain things were seen as essential. I was blessed with a "dream" red Schwinn bicycle, and a whole bookcase of books ranging from nursery rhymes to college-level classics.

One of my fondest memories is that of my mother flying into a parent-teacher conference with me in tow, her strawberry-blond hair and blue-green (one blue and one green) eyes on fire. She waved my neatly handwritten theme at my teacher. "What is this," she demanded, jabbing a bright red nail at the note my teacher had scrawled across the page. "What book did you copy this from???" the teacher's note said.

"I want you to know that my daughter does *not* need to plagiarize," my mother said in her "you-better-

123

listen-to-me" voice. "She has been writing since she was seven years old."

Whew. That was true. But here is something even more interesting. Only 7 years later I received a "D" in my college creative writing class. Only after I put in the effort to rewrite my first book seven times did I even begin to sense what has made the elite writers of all ages. It is a mountain of endless hours of rework.

In short, a natural gift is absolutely NO guarantee of success. Something called "dedicated action" has to be added to the recipe!

YOU Have Genius Potential

It's commonly assumed that "genius" equals a certain score on a standardized IQ test – and that either you're born a genius, or you're not. Is this long-accepted myth true?

Doctor Allie Sainy, a psychologist with the American Mensa Society, disagrees strongly with this old belief. She says, "A true genius may not score particularly well on a standard IQ test. We know a Nobel Prize winner who never scored at the Mensa level on a school IQ test – he was too busy seeing all the alternate possibilities for each answer."

So if genius is NOT a score on an IQ test, and NOT a born characteristic, what is it?

Dr. Anders Ericsson, a Florida State University professor says, "It's complicated explaining how genius or expertise is created and why it's so rare. But it isn't magic and it isn't born. It makes me think that even the most ordinary among us should be careful about saying we can't do great things, because it's been proven again and again that most people can do something extraordinary IF they're willing to put in the work."

What IS Genius?

Let's dive right into the mystery of genius, what it really is, and how YOU can tap into your own natural genius. When you think of someone's intelligence, what pops into your mind? Their IQ score? Then here is a surprise! Having genius-level IQ definitely does not necessarily lead to brilliant achievements.

A group of 157 graduates of New York City's Hunter College Elementary School with average IQ's of 157 (well into the "genius IQ" level) were studied later in life. Researcher Dr. Rena Subotnik was shocked to find that not one of these "geniuses" had any unusual levels of life achievement.

On the other hand several studies of writers, artists and musicians with presumed "genius-level talent" delivered another yet surprise – these "assumed geniuses" were found to have only above average IQs ranging from 115 to 130.

Interesting! At least 15% of the population has above average IQ scores. So how did those merely "above average" writers, artists and musicians develop genius level talent?

The obvious conclusion is that they must have worked harder. They might have been born with an above-average gift or potential, but only became elite genius-level achievers BECAUSE they made a serious commitment to develop their brain-based gift.

The 10-Year Rule

Columbia University's Eric Kandel won a Nobel Prize for discovering how our human brains learn and remember. His work proved that practice increases the number and strength of brain-cell-to-brain-cell connections tied to a skill.

Today most neuroscientists agree that "geniuses" are simply ordinary people who have worked to develop their brains.

What do these people do that lets them become geniuses?

Back in 1985 University of Chicago psychologist Benjamin Bloom completed a study of 120 elite achievers – top athletes, artists, performers, scientists and mathematicians. Dr. Bloom found that every one of them had spent at least ten years of committed work to reach their levels of achievement.

"Genius" is a set of exceptional skills that are created through disciplined study. Geniuses are *made*, not born!

Are Genius Brain's Different?

But what about the physical brains of geniuses? Are they somehow different? Let's take a look at this possibility.

As a child, Albert Einstein was seriously dyslexic. He had great difficulty learning to speak and read, and was considered an "impossible learner" by his teachers. He flunked his first college entrance exam,but finally did manage to get in and complete his bachelor's degree. Then only sixteen years later, Einstein was awarded the Nobel Prize for his brilliant theoretical physics work.

When Einstein died in 1955 Dr. Thomas Harvey, a pathologist on duty at Princeton Hospital, removed

Dr. Jill Ammon-Wexler

his brain. Harvey studied it under a microscope for 40 years, but never reported finding any differences from normal brains.

Then in the early 1980s Dr. Marian Diamond, a brilliant neuro-anatomist at the University of California Berkeley, revolutionized our ideas about what genius really is. Diamond placed a group of rats in a very stimulating environment with ladders, swings, treadmills, and rat toys. She also placed another group of rats in bare cages.

Dr. Marion Diamond

The stimulated rats lived to a healthy old age equal to 90 human years. But even more remarkable, the stimulated also rats grew an amazing number of new connections between their brain cells. What can we learn from Dr. Diamond's rat studies?

She had discovered the first hard evidence that intelligence can be increased using mentally-stimulating exercise.

Then when she then examined sections of Einstein's brain, she found that it truly *was* different from the "average" brain. Like her super-stimulated rats, Einstein's brain also had an unusually high number of experience-created brain cell connections.

So thanks to Dr. Diamond, another piece of the puzzle fell into place. We now know that geniuses are likely to have connection-rich brains that were developed through their own mentally stimulating efforts.

You Can <u>Build</u> Your Brain

Even if you are an "IQ-based genius," you're still FAR more intelligent than you think. There are proven ways to develop your brain's capacity for genius-level performance.

Remember the studies of Einstein's brain? His brain was different from "normal" brains in basically only one way: he had more enrichment-based connections among his brain cells.

On the brain-level, we now know that genius seems to be at least partially about such brain-cell-to-brain-cell connections.

Dr. Jill Ammon-Wexler

But having a genius-level density of brain cell connections is not a born condition. Such a "connection rich" brain is *created.*

Appropriate mental stimulation literally forces your brain to create new pathways and increasingly complex connections. John von Neumann, the inventor of the computer, estimated our brains hold two hundred and eighty quintillion bits of memory. That's the number 280 followed by 18 zeros. And this estimate is now considered too low. In short, you've got lot to work with!

Brain scans have clearly shown that every time you learn something new, you make entirely new and unique physical changes in your brain.

☆ The evidence is that the more you stimulate and challenge your brain, the more connections it creates. And the more unique connections you have, the closer you move toward creating your own personal genius-level brain.

The Really **BIG** Secret

You may still wonder just how Albert Einstein solved those "unsolvable" scientific questions and forever changed our understanding of the nature of life. Or how Pablo Picasso created entirely new images in art, or how a business leader like Bill Gates gets the insight that literally changed the world forever?

What is the special magic that makes one person an elite performer in their field – while others fail to even approach their true potential?

You have already learned about the ten-year rule and creating a connection-rich brain. But there are people who practice for over ten years and still never become elite achievers. Why? There's obviously something else at work.

Here's a clue: The date is August 23, 2006. We're in the Press Room at the WGC-Bridgestone Invitational Golf Tournament. Joel Schuchmann, the media room coordinator, is interviewing golfer Tiger Woods at the top of his game.

Schuchmann: "Can you talk a little bit about your mental toughness? It just seems like the great athletes have the ability to almost will things to happen. When you're that dialed in, do you feel like you can will things to happen?"

Woods: "Well, I think that your mind will carry you. The mind controls the body, so if the mind tells the body what to do, it'll do it. (It's) just a matter of getting the mind under control. And under the most extreme circumstances when the competition is that fierce and that heightened and my concentration is that high, yeah, I feel like I can make things happen." Can this ability be developed? YES!

Develop a "Varied Intelligence"

There's actually a whole new understanding of intelligence unfolding today. New research now finds other forms of intelligence are more important than IQ in terms of our real day-to-day living. These forms of intelligence include: Common sense, experience, intuition, emotional intelligence, creativity, and social intelligence – your ability to work well with others.

Many experts argue that it is these talents and not the limited skills measured by IQ tests that mark an intelligent person.

The business world agrees. Today many companies measure a potential executive's EQ (Emotional Intelligence Quotient) to determine their leadership potential. IQ is seen as far less meaningful. The concept of EQ is having quite an impact on the corporate world today.

Many companies are bringing in psychologists and coaches to improve their top executives' EQ.

Researchers say those with a strong EQ have far greater productivity, creativity, self-esteem and self-confidence – plus are more effective leaders. Worldwide studies find those with a high EQ have more success rising to the top of corporations. And in the case of independent entrepreneurs, a high EQ signals a higher probability of financial success.

EQ covers competency in optimism, effective productivity, self-esteem, motivation, empathy and personal interaction skills. The good news is this – your EQ can be dramatically increased.

Your "Emotional Smarts"

In the 1990s the concept of emotional intelligence exploded onto the scene almost overnight with the publication of a book by science writer Daniel Goldman – *Emotional Intelligence.*

What is the difference between IQ and emotional intelligence (EQ)? Your IQ is a measure of your analytical intelligence. Your EQ, on the other hand, is a measure of a far more practical intelligence related to your ability to understand your own and other's emotions.

Women and men tend to have equal EQs, but the sexes are stronger in different areas. Women score high in empathy and social responsibility, while men score higher in stress tolerance and self-confidence.

133

Dr. Jill Ammon-Wexler

But neither IQ nor EQ explain the full richness of our human intelligence, our capability to think "outside the box," our experiences of higher states and inspiration, and the deep levels of intuition some call ESP.

Your Higher Intelligence

Have you ever had the sensation of a light bulb flashing in your head? You were probably experiencing a sudden higher intelligence (HQ) breakthrough or insight.

What is HQ? We have come to what I consider to be the most exciting aspect of intelligence. Your HQ is much, much smarter than your logical IQ thinking.

The discovery of this powerful form of human intelligence began in the 1990s when two brilliant neurologists, Wolf Singer and Rodolfo Llinas, first began to investigate the mysterious electro-magnetic fields in our brains.

Their research led to the discovery of a surprising phenomenon that causes your entire cortex to vibrate in one coherent frequency. This remarkable experience happens during spontaneous insights and higher states of consciousness. And yes, you really may feel like a light bulb is flashing in your brain, or the top of your head is "buzzing" or "shaking" when you tap into your HQ.

Today's exciting brain scan research shows that those mysterious internal flashes of light and vibrations are tied to HQ – the higher intelligence you use to seek the ultimate levels of human consciousness.

Ultimately, your HQ allows you to create meaning in your life, to reach beyond the limits of both IQ and EQ, and to experience deeply transformational insights and experiences. It is at the core of your most inventive and creative moments, and also creates your "ah ha" insights and spiritual and higher meaning experiences.

Build Your HQ

Just like building the strength of your muscles, HQ is built through frequent use. One certain way to build

Dr. Jill Ammon-Wexler

your HQ is to seek deeper answers to the meaning of life. This requires challenging your own beliefs and assumptions – forcing your HQ to spring into action.

⭐ **Build your HQ by thinking about the following questions:**

Q. What is the meaning of my life?

Q. How does what's happening in the world impact me?

Q. What makes my life worth living?

Q. How do I want to be "remembered?"

You can begin to activate your HQ by first exhausting your ability to create *logical* answers to these questions.

Then when your brain reaches the point of exhaustion, just give up. Forget the question and take a nap or go for a walk. This will often bring a wholly unexpected HQ insight, although not necessarily immediately.

Albert Einstein had so many HQ insights in the shower that he always kept waterproof writing materials handy.

Wrap Up

You now realize that your brain contains the seeds of genius. You have personal potentials so far beyond what you are achieving today it's virtually staggering. Yes. I am talking about YOUR amazing brain and YOUR amazing untapped potential!

YOU have the capability to develop the complex mind of a genius, a Fortune 500 President, a great artist – whatever. This is entirely your choice, and within your control. And this has nothing to do with formal education, age, or personal background. You can use your own brain to create quantum leaps into an exciting new personal reality.

☆ Once you contemplate the following facts, your brain power will be permanently altered. The new brain-cell-to-brain-cell connections that are built while absorbing the implications of this knowledge will change your physical brain – forever.

This is comparable to walking on fire. You really will *never* be the same again.

You Have Unlimited Brain Power. Your brain absorbs an estimated 7 to 10 new pieces of information every second – and can continue to do so for the rest of your life. Each time you have a new experience or learn something, your brain physically

137

creates new brain cell connections. It's actually so growth-friendly that this process has a new scientific name – brain plasticity.

Your Cortex is Wrinkled for a Reason. Ever wonder why your cerebral cortex is such a mass of wrinkles? This is nature's answer to "high density housing." You have billions and billions of brain cells packed into your 3-pound brain. If all of your brain cells were laid out end-to-end, they would stretch at least 800,000 kilometers or 496,000 miles – a truly amazing distance.

Your Brain Extends Beyond Your Skull. Your intelligence actually spreads all the way down to each individual cell in your body. The body-mind barrier does NOT exist. You are a thinking being on every level. There is even a current scientific theory your brain is a holograph that is duplicated right down to a sub-molecular level. You are actually intelligence in action.

You Are Totally Unique. Of the six billion people currently living, and the ninety billion people who have ever walked the Earth, there has never been a person (or a brain) quite like yours. Your brain is as unique as your fingerprint. You are truly unprecedented and totally unique. Think about that!

You Have Unlimited Thoughts. Back in 1968 a student of the great Pavlov shocked the scientific community. His research proved that the human brain is capable of an unthinkable number of different thought patterns. His calculation revealed our potential to create unique thought patterns equaling the number 1 followed by 10.5 million kilometers of typewritten zeros. If you think in miles, this equals the number 1 followed by 6.55 million miles of typewritten zeros.

You Are Smarter Than Your IQ. Your intelligence transcends your IQ score. Neuro scientists and neuro psychologists now know that IQ tests only measure very limited "rational and logical" thinking skills. These skills are in many ways the most limited portion of your intelligence.

We now know there are also your emotional intelligence (EQ) and your higher intelligence (HQ). And many researchers now identify as many as 25 additional sub-intelligences – right down to the tactile intelligence of an artist, and the movement intelligence of a dancer.

Your Brain Can Grow. Recent research shows that one major thing setting Einstein's brain apart was the number of his brain-cell-to-brain-cell connections. This is not a birth condition. Such a densely packed brain is actually created by challenging yourself mentally – just like Einstein did.

Your Genes Do Not Limit You. An in-depth review of more than 200 scientific studies of IQ performed by researcher Bernard Devlin (published in "Nature journal") revealed that your genes account for only about 48 percent of your intelligence.

The remaining 52% percent is a function of your prenatal care, environment, and education. And this includes education at any age! Although your early upbringing and genetic background may make you inclined to have certain natural talents, research shows that your intelligence can be increased through appropriate training.

This Has <u>Already</u> Changed Your Brain

Just reading the previous information created *immediate* changes in your brain. Now if you actually spend a little time contemplating what these insights mean to you, you will immediately strengthen those new brain connections even more.

The stronger they get, the more easily they will overrule any old limiting thoughts about your own potential for genius-level living.

NINE. FIRE UP EMOTION

You're at work trying to finish a project. The pressure is on, and you are up to your elbows in project paperwork. There is no time for even a short break. Two coworkers stroll by with aromatic cups of coffee from the nearby Starbucks. "Messy desk," one of the women comments to the other as they stroll past your desk.

A sudden rush of heat rolls up your neck and onto your face. You squeeze your fists to control yourself. You logically know your anger is overblown, but you still feel an impulse to let loose with a barrage of salty words. "Wow. She really has no concept!" you hiss through clamped teeth.

A few hours later you finish your project. You now have two minutes to straighten up your workspace and get out the door to beat the rush hour traffic. You scoop your paperwork together, shove it into an empty folder, and open the drawer where you keep your car keys.

No keys. You feel in your pockets – still no keys. You are still tearing through one desk drawer after another as the office begins to empty out. You now face an extra 30 minutes peak traffic drive time, and still no keys. Your anxiety heats up another notch.

A co-worker notices your panic and walks over. "Hey," he asks, "is something wrong?"

You explain.

"Where do you normally keep your keys?" he asks. You point to your middle desk drawer. He opens the drawer and pulls out your keys. "Are these yours?" he asks.

They are, of course. But you looked in that same drawer and truly did not see them there. What went wrong?

Emotion Controls Our Behavior

Do you recall being told as a child to "control yourself?" What was that demand in reference to? Your emotional expression, of course. So were you able to do as requested?

If you've ever tried to control or repress an emotion (and we all have) you recall it took some physical action – perhaps clamping your jaws tight, holding your breath, tightening your stomach, etc.

☆ The idea that emotions can be controlled using logic and willpower is totally wrong. Emotions are actually a physical response to chemicals released by your brain's emotional center *BEFORE* the logical part of your brain can even begin to intervene.

Have you ever tried to use logic to control a strong emotion? Then you know how hard it is to be logical and calm when the hair is up on the back of your neck, your scalp is crawling, your fists are clenched, and you can feel the heat rising up into your face.

Logic does not enable you to control your emotions for a reason. Emotions are *NOT* just in your mind.

Each emotion immediately floods your body with chemicals released by your brain. No amount of logic can turn such a tide. Emotions are a bodily event. They are not just a mental phenomenon.

When you "stuff" an emotion, what you are doing is fighting back against very real chemicals surging though your bloodstream.

Why Emotions Rule

Emotions are the driving force behind all of our behavior and responses to everything happening around or inside of us.

Emotions rule your behavior for a reason. Their power is built right into how your physical brain is arranged. Remember the tiger story? Then you recall that your RAS (your brain's "emotional crisis center") has a few milliseconds of lead time before that same "I see a tiger" message reaches your higher thinking center – your cortex. This means you're already in the middle of an emotional response before your thinking brain is even aware of what's happening.

This is why you cannot just think an emotion away. Emotions run right over your brain's logical thinking center. Your cortex simply does not reach down into your emotional brain (your limbic center) as fast as the emotional brain sends signals up into your higher thinking centers.

So your emotions are ALWAYS in control first, and your logical mind only comes in second.

Emotions Are Basically Habits

The manner in which you express your emotions is based on hard-wired habits that you learned in childhood.

Maybe you were taught to hold your emotions in and "go to your room" when angry or frustrated. If so, this is now at the core of how you handle your anger or feelings or frustration today.

Your old emotional habits can resist change. But remember, habits are just learned behaviors. Anything that has been learned can be relearned. It does take determination, but you can change how you express your emotions.

Many psychologists say it takes twenty-one days to create a new habit. But actually you move forward in the fraction of a second during which you *decide* to do so. Your decision is the most important part of the process. And the more intense the emotion linked to your decision, the faster you will achieve your goal. Emotion is e-motion – energy in motion.

Emotions and Goals

Did you realize that emotion is the driving force behind most of your thoughts and actions? In fact, emotions and action are so intimately connected they truly cannot be separated.

Emotion is also at the very core of your goals – which are simply emotional commitments to what you want to do and who you want to become. Your emotions, in turn, are shaped by your beliefs – by what you tell yourself is possible. Nobel Prize winning scientist Dr. Candace Pert calls emotions "the glue that holds the cells of the organism together."

Dr. Jill Ammon-Wexler

The challenge is to use your emotional energy in use a constructive way. Positive emotions broaden your thinking and build your intellectual and social effectiveness. They also support creative and flexible thinking. Negative emotions, on the other hand, constrict and limit creativity – and thus reduce the chance you will achieve your goals.

Emotions and Stress

Stress is emotion plus! The stress response is basically designed to rapidly get you out of harm's way. Remember the story about "seeing" the eyes of an escaped tiger watching you from behind a bush? The intense physical and mental reaction you felt when you "saw" those eyes is an example of stress in action.

Stress causes you to focus down in your brain stem – the part of your brain that is strongly dedicated to your survival. That's perfect if survival is actually an issue. But if you are trying to use your higher thinking centers, forget it.

Science now knows that stress causes your higher brain to shut down. Your hippocampus (the part of your brain that assembles memories) also tends to dysfunction under stress. That's why people often cannot remember their own address when making an emergency 911 phone call – or why you can't find your car keys when you're rushed.

⭐ As stress becomes more intense your brain cells begin to physically shrivel up. And if your stress becomes chronic, your brain cells actually begin to die, and portions of your brain begin to shrink. There is no doubt we live in an increasingly stressful world today, so it's important to learn to take control.

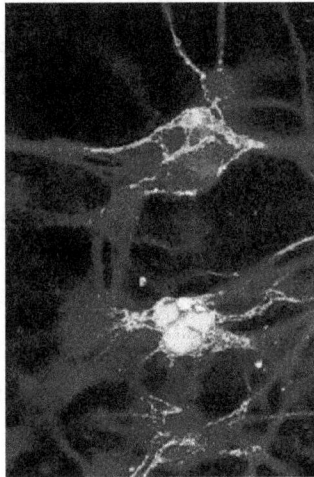

Neurons (brain cells) dying
from an intense stress overload.

Using the Emotion of Anger

We all experience strong emotions – they're a shared aspect of our human nature and condition. But what's less common is a conscious decision to *use* emotions to expand one's self.

147

Dr. Jill Ammon-Wexler

There are five emotional states that can help you take quantum leaps forward in your life: Anger, decision, commitment, focus and passion. Are you surprised to find anger at the front of the list? Interestingly, anger often activates the other four – decision, commitment, focus and passion.

Here's a real life example:

Joe Martinelli has held the same job as a graphic artist in the marketing department of a mid-sized Sydney Australia company for almost four years. His manager praises his work and frequently asks for his advice on the work of four junior graphic artists. Joe is looking forward to filling the new position of Graphic Manager that has just opened up.

It's Friday afternoon and his boss calls him into the office. Joe figures this is it – his promotion. Joe's boss compliments him on his latest project, but then starts to chew his lip. He clears his throat to break the silence. "Joe," he finally says. "I'm afraid I have some bad news. I hate to say this, but upper management didn't take my recommendation. They hired someone from the outside to fill the Graphic Manager position."

Joe blinks and swallows hard. "But, I've been here for almost four years and..."

"I'm sorry Joe," his manager sighed. "It's out of my hands. He's starting in two weeks, and we have to move you out into the art bay so he can have your office."

An overwhelming mix of painful, angry emotions keeps Joe awake all night. Not only was he passed over for promotion, but he is being "demoted" to sit in the art bay with the junior artists.

His anger and frustration multiply over the weekend. By Monday morning Joe is boiling over with anger. He pulls into the parking lot and sits in the car watching the other employees stream into the building.

His thoughts turn to a friend of his – an illustrator who recently quit his job and became a free-lancer. "Lucky stiff," he mumbles. Suddenly Joe feels a light bulb go off in his head. "That's it," he snaps. "Enough is enough."

Joe marches into his boss' office and hands him a scribbled two-week notice that he's quitting.

Joe is today the owner of one of Australia's most successful "temp" businesses. His specialty is providing the services of other creative artists, writers and designers on a "for fee" basis.

149

His anger was his motivator! Joe arrived at this great place in his life because he came to a fork in the road, made a choice, then took action. His experience contains the secret of how emotion can drive you forward in *YOUR* life. The components of his success were anger, decision, commitment, focus and passion.

☆ We each arrive at such forks in the road, and our resulting decisions set the course of our lives. When you reach such a fork you will recognize it because of the accompanying emotional turmoil – a *natural* part of change and growth.

The best advice is to just choose a direction and take action. It's far more productive to make a wrong turn than to just sit on the fence. And if your decision does not take you where you want to go, you can always make a new decision.

For example, Joe could have turned onto any number of forks. He could have just hunkered down, signed up for a management degree from an on-line university, changed his career focus, or asked for a transfer to another division of the company.

Create Emotional Flow

We basically have two choices of how to experience our emotions:

1. Express them outwardly, or

2. Repress them and stuff them down inside.

Most social groups (beginning with the family) place definite limits on how much emotional expression is acceptable, and orced emotionally repression is unfortunately very common.

Many of us learned as children that no matter how much someone might upset you, openly venting your rage or frustration might only make things worse. So we might have learned to repress our emotions to avoid possible judgment, scolding, punishment, or even rejection.

But when emotion is repressed, the associated mental and physiological energy does *NOT* just go away. We don't stop having emotions. There is no way to prevent the arousal of emotional energy in response to life any more than we can prevent our heart from beating.

Instead our emotions just sink deeper. Emotional repression then becomes an unconscious habit. And closing down your emotional energy dampens your ability to respond effectively to life – to think and act creatively, spontaneously, and decisively. It also damages your ability to communicate with and understand other people – shutting down an

Dr. Jill Ammon-Wexler

important component of your emotional intelligence (EQ).

A Better Choice

There's a third choice beyond uncontrolled emotional expression or repression.

You have probably heard athletes speak of being "in the flow." Being "in the flow" is a state that allows you to effortlessly achieve optimal performance. And here is the good news – this can also be achieved with your emotional expression.

Emotional "flow" is not uncontrolled or repressed emotional expression. It is a learned method of emotional expression based on refined personal *choice.*

The three secrets to creating emotional flow in your life include: (1) Attitude flexibility, (2) the ability to relax, and (3) refined breathing skills.

Attitude Flexability. The first secret to developing emotional flow is making a commitment to use your emotional energy to better serve your own well being. This starts with a decision to be flexible and accept whatever is happening around and inside you.

I am not saying you necessarily enjoy or agree with what is happening. You might dislike some people, the weather, or your job very much. But no matter how much you dislike something or someone, you DO have a choice:

Imagine yourself in a kayak in a turbulent, rushing river full of huge rocks. You have no time to think – you must simply accept the danger of the wild roaring water and the rocks. There is no time to wish you were somewhere else, and no hope of changing the direction and flow of the water.

You have two choices: Either let the water control you, or get your hands on a paddle and take control. Emotion-packed situations are like that.

Given a choice, wouldn't you rather have a paddle in your hands than just be swept along by the water and thrown onto the rocks? With a paddle you can create a measure of control over what's happening.

What am I suggesting?

Try accepting what is happening around you, but actively go with the flow. Use your emotional power as a paddle to steer yourself through any challenging situations. Do not just let life sweep you along as a passive observer or victim, while just stuffing all your emotional power and being smashed against the rocks.

The important lesson is to accept – and *then* use your e-motion power to create positive change.

The Ability to Relax. The second secret of positive emotional flow is active physical relaxation. Repressed emotion creates physical tension in your body that can quickly become chronic. Medical science tells us that stress is a major creator of disease, and both repressed and out-of-control emotions are the source of much of our physical and mental stress.

Active relaxation is quite different from using drugs or alcohol, or collapsing in front of the TV. These may relieve your tension, but do so by dampening your level of awareness. Such relaxation comes at a "quality of life" price.

You can experience far more positive relaxation in a number of ways: From deep meditation to mentally stimulating mental work, a regular practice of yoga or tai chi, a massage, a good physical workout, gardening, good, loving contact, or engineered brainwave training. But one of the fastest ways to deep relaxation is good breathing practives.

Good Breathing Practices. Early in life we discover that some of our emotions irritate our parents and other caregivers. And we may also discover that we can often stop the outward expression of an emotion by just holding our breath. Many researchers believe this is a direct cause of childhood asthma.

However breathing can ALSO be a very powerful tool for positively directing your emotions. Breathing affects your nervous system and can shut off the stress response. The secret is to create a gentle, flowing breath pattern. Start by becoming aware of your breathing, and then consciously settle into a slower, more relaxed pattern.

As your breathing slows you will automatically feel more relaxed and in control. This simple step alone moves you toward a state of positive emotional flow, and helps create the Alpha brainwaves associated with stress-free deep relaxation.

Put Emotion to Work

Now that you have a new appreciation of the power of emotion, how about putting it to work to better

Dr. Jill Ammon-Wexler

achieve your goals? What follows is a plan of action to get your emotion working for you:

Use Your Amygdale. The amygdale in your brain's limbic system are a secret to why fear is such a powerful emotional force. But your amygdale can also be used to focus your brain on positive goals and desires.

When you have a passion to achieve a goal, your amygdale will actually physically create an active focus on your desire in your learning and memory center – your brain's hippocampus.

This can cause you to become "possessed" by an unstoppable burning desire to achieve your goal. And since your hard-working hippocampus will hold that desire right in the front of your memory banks, it will seem as though almost everything reminds you to pursue your goal.

☆ This is the brain-based reason success is inevitable if you set goals you have a passionate desire to achieve. The key is positive burning passion!

We now know from quantum physics that nothing is fixed – that there really are no limitations and virtually everything is potential. Everything, including you, is truly in the process of becoming. Become more by using your passion.

Set Your Intentions. Stay focused on what you want in order to keep your emotion and motivation pumped. Because of the way your brain is wired, what you focus on will grow and expand. Remember to focus on what you want, not on what stands in your way!

"OK," I can hear you ask. "So how can I quit focusing on the problems that are flying in my face?"

One of the things neuroscience tells us is this: There is only a tiny fraction of a second of time between the time you "see" something that reminds you of an imminent problem – and your *choice* of how you will interpret and respond to that problem.

Focusing on what you *want* will push your brain to make the choices you want to make!

Watch Your Thoughts. Suppose you want to buy a house, but have been turned down again and again for financing. You now have an ANT running through your mind every time you even think of buying a house. The message? "It's no use. Just forget it. No one in the family has ever owned a home anyway."

157

Dr. Jill Ammon-Wexler

One day a friend tells you about an abandoned house that's for sale in his neighborhood. The house is owned by an older man who just wants to get rid of it.

Your brain is going to want to immediately activate an "it's no use" ANT. You have a fraction of a second to instead get motivated and act on the opportunity. What makes the difference between "passing on it" and "grabbing the opportunity?" The ability to DO something about your mental focus is what makes the difference.

Adjust Your Focus. OK. You've discovered you can't get financing. So maybe your focus on "buy" needs to be adjusted to "own." What if you use that fraction of a second to replace that ANT with a new message? What if that new message is, "I am capable of *owning* a house."

And what if in that fraction of a second you choose to hold your focus on that positive thought and short-circuit the "just forget it" ANT for now?

You jump into action, contact the owner, and offer to solve his problem. You will move in and do repairs at your own expense if he agrees to count the repairs as the down payment. He will then finance the rest and have a steady stream of money for retirement.

The owner agrees. Instead of banging your head against what you don't want, you used that fraction of a second to get what you *do* want.

Install Positive Beliefs. Remember it is not what's happening around you, but how you *interpret* it, that creates your reality. You will benefit greatly by installing emotionally positive beliefs into your brain to keep yourself motivated.

Winston Churchill said, "Success is going from failure to failure without loss of enthusiasm." Your enthusiasm for life (or lack of it) maps the direction of your future. Turn the tide by installing some new positive beliefs into your mind today.

Dr. Jill Ammon-Wexler

TEN. THE SECRET OF MOTIVATION

Have you heard of the "carrot" method of motivation? The basic assumption is that we humans have a lot in common with donkeys. Hook up a carrot on a stick in front of a donkey and it will pull your cart. The assumption is that the promise of a reward is the best motivator.

This does sound a lot like the method our parents used on us as kids – the "take out the garbage and you'll get a cookie technique." What really pushes you out of bed in the morning and off to work? And what is really behind achieving or not achieving your goals? Is it more than just the promise of a carrot or cookies?

Have you ever felt you truly wanted to do something – perhaps lose some weight or get a new job – but found it impossible to stay motivated? Or maybe you started your own business, but when your cash flow dropped you gave up and closed up shop? Or perhaps you feel like you are making the same old communication or creative mistake over and over and over again?

What's behind this?

Understanding Motivation

Back in the 1940 era an American psychologist, Dr. Abraham Maslow, came up with a clearly brilliant explanation of motivation.

His explanation is so clear you will immediately "get it." Although Maslow was not an expert on how the brain works, his theory makes sense in terms of what *you* now know about the brain.

Maslow's model can be interpreted very easily: He believed that until we satisfy a lower level of "needs" portrayed in the form of a pyramid, we are simply NOT motivated to seek the next higher level, or step

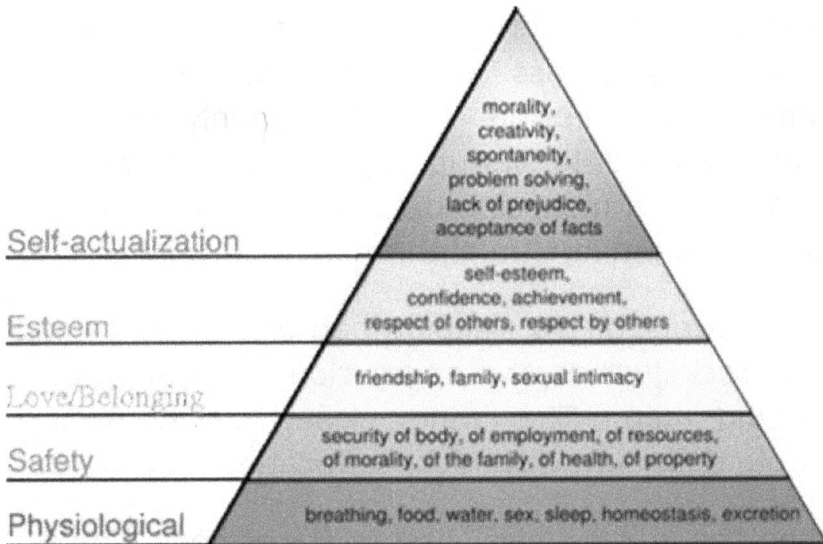

Maslow's Hierarchy of Human Needs

A "Needs" Story

Harry Martin, age 42 and from Seattle, is camping by himself several miles out into the Sahara desert – a longtime dream. Harry is an experienced camper and hiker, and feels well equipped for his personal quest.

Harry has come to the Sahara to seek some personal answers. He has been struggling with how to pay off an alarming credit card debt, and also how to climb the next rung of the corporate ladder at work and get a substantial raise.

He rolls out his sleeping bag under the clear desert sky and gazes up at the stars. Sleep comes easily.

Dr. Jill Ammon-Wexler

Harry is suddenly torn from sleep as a violent gust of sand blows across his face. He rolls over in momentary confusion … then suddenly remembers where he's at. He sits up to find the clear night sky replaced by a menacing dark cloud rolling across the sand, and coming straight at him.

He leaps out of his sleeping bag and dives behind a large rock just as the angry cloud carries away his sleeping bag. The wind closes down on him, surrounding him with thick, suffocating blackness.

When the storm finally passes Harry finds himself in a bizarre wind-sculpted landscape of shifting sand dunes. The sun is barely visible behind the murky blanket of sand and dust hanging in the air. There's no trace of the road he followed out. All of his water, food and survival gear has been blown away, or buried beneath tons of sand.

His overwhelming credit card debt and climbing the corporate ladder are suddenly unimportant. Harry is motivated by one thing alone – an immediate need to ensure his physical survival. He must find water, food and some form of shelter! Harry is now totally focused in his brain's survival center – the brain stem.

Q. Will He Survive? Harry has totally lost his bearings. The sky is still clogged with sand, and all traces of the previous landscape are gone. He gives up digging in the sand trying to find his gear, and realizes he has to find a source of water – now! He is definitely heavily focused on the first level of Maslow's needs pyramid – the "Physiological" Level,

Harry scans the dusty skyline and sees what looks like a faint outline of a group of trees. "Were those there yesterday?" he mumbles. "Not sure." He sets his teeth and sets out for what he hopes is an oasis.

Two hours later he collapses onto his knees and falls face down in a tiny pool of water. Luck is on his side. A date palm was uprooted in the wind and a small clump of ripe dates is still attached. He now has water, food, and some shelter from the sun. He has now satisfied the basic needs of the lowest level of Maslow's motivational pyramid—the need for immediate physiologically survival.

Q. Is His Continued Safety Certain? Harry is OK for now. But what about tomorrow? He is now motivated to climb up onto the next step of the pyramid – to seek a sense of security that his survival needs will CONTINUE to be met. We've come upon the instinct to "plan for our future survival."

Is this an instinct? Yes! The entire animal kingdom plans for the future. Birds build nests. Bears plan for hibernation. Squirrels stash nuts for the winter. Spiders seek out warm places to nest from the rain or cold.

We humans have the same drive. But this drive does not engage our higher brain centers. The survival-level stress Harry faces still has him focused down in the lower part of his brain – the brain stem.

By the next morning the sky has cleared and Harry finally gets his bearings from the direction of the sunrise. Then he spots what could be flashes of sunlight off car windshields. "The road?"

He fills his stomach with water, soaks his t-shirt and wraps it around his head, and sets off toward the flashes of light. A few hot hours later he reaches the road. That afternoon he's on a plane, exhausted and sun burnt, but headed home to Seattle. Harry's physiological survival-level needs have now been met. So, one day later, He is again worrying about how to get that big raise he needs to pay off his credit card debt.

We naturally have a deep motivation to be sure we'll be able to survive tomorrow. When that ability is uncertain, we can become very anxious and stressed. And as you now know, stress shuts down your higher thinking centers – throwing you down into the less intelligent portions of your brain. Harry is still locked into Maslow's second level – safety.

Although his physical survival is no longer an issue, concern over survival of high credit card debt and a need for a higher income is creating worry and stress that locks Harry into his brain stem and emotional limbic center.

Q. Does He Belong? Harry gets a raise, and now feels confident of his ability to provide for the future. So what comes next? Now a more thorny aspect of our "human nature" comes into play. We humans are primarily "tribal" creatures. The next thing that motivates Harry is a desire for a sense of "comfort and belonging." Like most of us, he wants to feel connected to others.

He begins to spend more time with like-minded people. So now Harry is out of the desert and with a solid sense of future security. He also has a couple of pals, belongs to the biking club, and feels like he is part of the team at work.

A sense of belonging builds an inward sense of emotional security in the important emotional center of our brain – the limbic center. People who do not have the ability to satisfy this need often suffer from emotional pain, loneliness and depression.

167

Q. Does He Like Himself? Harry has come a long way from his desperate survival-level search for water, food and shelter. Now he can focus in an even higher level of his brain – his smart cerebral cortex.

He begins to ask himself some searching questions, and is now driven by a higher motivation – the desire to truly like and respect himself. He gets this through self-examination and self-appreciation. He has activated the positive feelings center in his left pre-frontal cortex.

And because we are basically social animals, Harry also looks to those he respects to validate his self-esteem. This further expands his EQ, his leadership and communication skills improve, and he gets his desired promotion

Q. Can He Expand Upward? OK. Harry has now survived his desert crisis, ensured improved financial survival, satisfied his social needs, and even created an improved sense of self-esteem.

What comes next? Harry is now ready to strive to reach the top of the pyramid -- what Maslow considered the pinnacle of human accomplishment.

He has become a "self-actualizing person" motivated to seek even more personal growth and meaning. He is now positively driven to rise above any personal "limitations," and to become all he can be in his lifetime.

What about his brain? Harry is now focusing a lot in his HQ – his higher intelligence. He is experiencing intense personal insights and higher consciousness experiences as his brain lights up mysterious higher cortical centers.

Move Up the Pyramid

Do you feel stuck at a lower level on Maslow's pyramid? Here are three ways to move up:

- **Check Your Focus.** Are you seeing only one side of a challenge or problem that seems to be holding you at lower "survival" levels? Can you focus on the possibility of a solution, or perhaps view your situation as a CHALLENGE, rather than as your reality?

  How would an intelligent optimist view your situation? How else can YOU view it? Ask yourself IF you are blaming some external person or thing, rather than claiming your own power to respond.

- **Give Yourself a Pep Talk.** When something goes wrong, pessimists tend to have hopeless thoughts and tons of ANTs crawling around in their minds. Avoid this and try to use positive

169

affirmations to put ANTs in their place. Reframe what you are saying to yourself and push your brain to "focus positive." Focus on solutions, rather than the problem. Remember – what you focus on will grow.

- **Take Some Time Out.** Studies show that if you think about a problem in a negative frame of mind, you are FAR less likely to come up with a solution. Give yourself some time out. Go do something you enjoy. Come back to your challenge more relaxed, more optimistic, and far more creative.

The "You" of the Future

Imagine walking into a room and meeting the YOU of ten years from today.

What do you look like? How are you dressed? Where are you living? What is your lifestyle? What car do you drive? Are you running a business? If so, how successful are you? What is your net worth? What have you invested in? Who is your mate? Who are your friends? Do you travel?

We humans are primarily driven to take action by two desires – experiencing pleasure, or avoiding pain. Tony Robbins feels that pain is a more powerful motivator than pleasure. I tend to agree with him.

You basically have three choices about how the "you of the future" will look. Your choices are:

- Somewhere in between how you are today and a broken down mess. Here's where an "avoid pain" motivator could kick in.

- An exact duplicate of how you are today, except ten years older. Absolutely nothing has changed in a decade. This is not a very satisfying picture for most of us, and could be a strong "avoid pain" motivator for many.

- A happier, healthier and more successful version of the you of today. This choice kicks in your "experience pleasure" motivator.

Choice One. You probably would NOT choose number one. But if that is the general direction of your life, there's still a positive way to put this to work. The fear of being a "broken-down mess" in ten years can create a hot and intense *avoid pain* message to help motivate you to take action. The secret? Use your wish to avoid pain as a *positive* motivator.

Choice Two. If you are moving toward choice two, you can expect that nothing will change over the next ten years. The you of 10 years in the future will be identical to today's you. So you will still face

171

today's problems and frustrations, but will have ten more years of them piled up.

Choice two is an active decision to remain in your comfort zone. But this is actually only make-believe safety. In today's rapidly changing world, the comfort zone is constantly being eroded from beneath your feet.

Choice Three. Choice three falls into the arena of dreams and wishes. If all our dreams would automatically come true, life would be truly sweet. But, unless you are very unusual, the problems and challenges of everyday life tend to take priority over your dreams.

The truth is, we each create our own reality and our own future. It all starts with our beliefs. But there is more involved than just "believing" we will somehow achieve our daydreams. Just holding a happy picture of some future life usually does not build the intense fire and desire required to create that desired lifestyle. *Dreams come true when we wake up and go to work.*

Use the Power of Attraction

I'm sure you've heard the expression, "the power of attraction." For the past 100 years or so, many writers have used this term to refer to a mysterious ability to manifest what we desire. It has been suggested that the real secret of manifesting is the power of attraction – an unexplained force created by simply focusing on what you desire.

Yes, there truly is a power of attraction, but you don't have to believe in magic to get it working in your life. The scientific explanation for how this works is very easy to understand.

The Brain-Based Power of Attraction. The true power of attraction comes from a *choice* to use your brain in a certain way. How? The amygdale in your brain's limbic system can be used to specifically focus your brain *away* from survival issues and threats, and to focus instead on your goals and desires.

If you have an intense passion for something, your amygdale will feed this directly into your learning and memory center – your brain's hippocampus. This is a major key to the true power of attraction. Your hippocampus will respond by building strong brain networks based on that intense emotional desire.

Remember? *Emotion is like cement that builds strong brain networks.*

That is why success becomes inevitable IF you have a passionate desire for it. The key is positive burning passion! This is a major reason affirmations work, and also why it's so important to focus intense positive emotions on your goals.

One proven-effective way to keep your brain tightly focused on a goal is to create a notebook or collage of pictures reflecting your desired goal. Looking at this often will help intensify your focus.

☆ Take Action

Get Started TODAY. Remember how you felt when you looked at the three choices of how your life will look in ten years? Get what you want in your life by putting your brain's motivation machine to work. Here are four steps to get you started TODAY:

1. Decide WHAT You Want. First, you have to clearly decide *exactly* what you want. Put all four of the following steps into a pie, and this step begins as 100 percent of the pie. Until you complete this step, the other three are totally meaningless.

Look at it this way. If you get into a cab and tell the driver you just want to go "someplace warm," you could end up anywhere from at home in your bed, at the airport waiting for a plane to Hawaii, or even in a local spa soaking in a hot tub. But if you tell him you want to go to 1243 Third Avenue West – you will end up exactly where you want to go.

Many people spend their lives dreaming of what they would like to have and be. They find their fulfillment in daydreams.

There is nothing wrong with daydreams. They actually play a major part in any real effort to get what you want.

However daydreams only come true when you wake up and go to work. And before you can go to work, you need to select from among your dreams and decide what you really want to have, do, or become. In short – what you are willing to commit your daily life energy to!

2. Determine WHERE You Are Right Now. Take another look at the illustration of Maslow's hierarchy of needs. Figure out where you are focused right now – TODAY.

If you are focused on Maslow's level of "Esteem Needs," it makes no sense to try to immediately leap to the highest level of "Self Actualization." Maslow taught that we tend to progress up the pyramid one step at a time.

So IF you are on the Esteem needs level, the way to move up is to focus on building your self esteem. *Then* UP YOU GO!

3. Know You DESERVE IT. Once you've truly decided what you want to do, have or be, the next step is to believe you deserve it.

This is where your subconscious mind comes into play. Your subconscious mind is a storehouse of everything that has happened to you over your entire life. You may not consciously remember being put down for your first business failure (a sidewalk lemonade stand), but your subconscious mind clearly remembers your older brother telling you "you're stupid for doing that."

Building a belief that you deserve something better can sometimes be a challenge because of ANTs. The minute some people try to believe they are worth more, their ANTs start to insist they do not deserve it because they're too dumb, too unworthy, too incapable, or too ... whatever.

⭐ One way to overcome feelings of not being worthy is to get really mad. Red hot anger at any so-called limitations can be a great motivator.

Anger is what both personal growth guru Tony Robbins and famous performer Tina Turner used to change their lives overnight.

So … if you feel stuck, fire up some anger to fuel positive action. It works! But then be sure to let go of the anger and put positive emotions to work.

4. BELIEVE In You. Next we move even deeper into the realm of belief. You can never believe you will have something new in your life unless you *first* believe in yourself. This requires that you figure out just who you are.

Many people spend their lives playing "hide and seek" with themselves, and do not put enough energy into the "seek" part of the game. You have heard the expression, "knowledge is power." Self-knowledge is the greatest success-building power of all.

YOU are the source of everything in your own life. Your hopes and your dreams all rest on you. You invest in your car, your home, your pets, your clothes, your entertainment. But are you investing ENOUGH in growing your own self?

This is an important step in reaching the level of success you *are* capable of. If you have a business or profession, for example, you have to grow yourself to grow your business. The same is true of being a successful entrepreneur or climbing the corporate ladder

5. Take ACTION.   Grow by taking action! Once you have taken all of the above steps, you are ready to make it happen in the world. But if you begin to take action before you complete steps 1 through 4, you may end up with the bitter taste of failure in your mouth.

If that's the case, go back to Step 1 and work your way down through the steps again. You owe it to yourself, and you ARE worth it. Just take action!

ELEVEN. FUTURE MEMORIES

The idea of creating "future memories" may seem odd, but it's a totally natural brain-based mental process. A future memory is basically a mental picture of you in a visualized future time. And the truth is you're creating such memories virtually every day.

"Why focus on this?" you might wonder. The answer may surprise you. By building "future memories" you do something truly remarkable – you actually pull yourself forward through time toward what you focus on.

Here's an example of how future memories work: Suppose you're out golfing with a friend at your favorite course. Your friend tees off with a fabulous long drive, and lands right on the green. You instantly recall the last time you shot for that green, and ended up in the trees. Your subconscious mind instantly gets the picture and sends a message to your brain's motor centers to create an identical shot.

179

Dr. Jill Ammon-Wexler

So, do you think your ball will end up on the green? Unlikely! You'll probably end up in the trees again. What happened? You created a future memory of your drive, and your subconscious mind interpreted your future memory as a action direction. You know the rest.

Suppose you want to create more success in your business, or perhaps improve your financial well being, but your subconscious mind is packed with emotional pictures of probable failure. What results do you think you can expect?

The interesting thing is, you actually use this process constantly. There's really no way to turn it off. You are constantly either creating future memories of success, *or* future memories of failure.

So if you feel like a failure, you will simply continue to fail. Your subconscious mind is just following instructions. There is only one way to break this pattern! You MUST create a new set of future memories and implant them solidly on the neural networks in your physical brain.

Future Memories Mold Behavior

Your powerful subconscious mind molds your every thought, feeling, emotion and action to correspond to your mental pictures. In this way, your mental pictures truly serve as your subconscious guidance system.

The way you react from moment to moment is *totally* consistent with this subconscious guidance system. It guides you toward actions and behaviors that will manifest the dreams and goals you picture with your future memories.

☆ Your daily reality is therefore a direct reflection of your future memories. Whatever you consciously or unconsciously focus on and project as an expectation for the future, whether positive or negative, will guide your beliefs and actions. This is actually a direct cause of almost every success and every failure.

This is why a better lifestyle must begin with an improvement to your future memories. People who are successful continually build and focus on a future memory of the life they want to lead. Unsuccessful people continually build and focus on future memories of what they do NOT want in their life. It really IS that simple!

Vision and Visualization

It's important to appreciate the fact that future memories are a *physical* brain reality. They are *not* just an imaginary psychological idea. To build this understanding, let's take a look at how your brain works. We'll start with the process of seeing, then consider how your brain processes what you visualize.

Vision is by far the most powerful and important of your physical senses. It allows you to image the world around you and make sense of your immediate environment.

Your vision is one of the most sensitive and complicated of all of your physical senses. A surprising 25% of your brain is actively involved in the complex process of seeing and interpreting what you see. In many ways, your eyes truly are a direct extension of your brain out into your external environment.

The Science of Vision

Each of your eyes has 125,000,000 visual receptors. These receptors are actually specialized neurons (you recall that neurons are the basic cells of the brain). And you likely also remember from your studies of biology in school that these specialized neurons in your eyes are called rods and cones.

But you may not realize what vision really IS. What your eyes actually see is ONLY light being reflected off the surface of something. That's it. What you actually see is only reflected light! You actually do *not* "see" objects.

Those special neurons in your eyes (the rods and cones) convert this reflected light into electrical signals that are then sent into your brain via your optic nerve. Your brain analyzes these tiny electrical signals, then uses them to send chemical messages to your brain cells (neurons). Y

our brain then uses these messages to create a mental picture of what you have seen. So when you say you see something, what you really "see" is only a mental picture that was actually assembled and created in your own brain.

The Art of "Visualization"

Creating a future memory is basically using your imagination (instead of your eyes) to create an <u>actual</u> brain image of "seeing" something. This creation of a picture in your mind (without actually seeing it with your eyes) is often commonly known as the process of "visualization."

Here's what's important: Just like actually <u>seeing</u> something with your eyes, a future memory creates the same <u>physical</u> electrical and chemical signals in your brain. In terms of your brain, the process of using mental imagery to create a future memory is

Dr. Jill Ammon-Wexler

just as real as your normal "seeing" process. If we review the reports of world class athletes and other super achievers, there's no doubt that this process is a powerful method of achieving goals and radically increasing one's performance.

What Science Says. Recent PET (positron-emission tomography) scans of healthy human brains have provided absolute positive proof that mental visualization of a complex movement (such as that involved in a sport) can help improve actual performance.

There's also research evidence that such improvements are *not* limited to sports activities. that Future memories can improve intellectual activities such as delivering a speech, playing music, acting, and even playing chess.

☆ Additional PET scan research has also clearly established that merely thinking about something brings about actual physical changes in the brain. Think about the implications of that for a moment.

Future memory imaging is "seeing" into the future. Instead of your brain interpreting light being reflected off an object, you're seeing a future memory of yourself performing some action, or achieving some goal or state of being, in the future.

Remarkable thought, isn't it? Plus as you strengthen your future memories by replaying them in your mind, the physical neural networks that hold these memories will continue to grow stronger and more stable.

Enter Your Subconscious Mind. Does it matter that what you are visualizing or mentally picturing as a future memory isn't "real" yet? Not at all. Your subconscious mind virtually *cannot* tell the difference between something you "see," and something you mentally picture as a future memory. And the more detailed your images of your future memories, the more robust will be the physical neural networks holding those memories.

So assuming you have a clear picture of your dream or goal, your next logical step is to begin to create some detailed future memories of how it looks *RIGHT NOW* to have already achieved it.

Such a seeing process requires that you clearly fill in the details of how it will be to have achieved that dream goal. The more detailed your vision, the better you'll be able to see it and achieve it.

If you want to build a new house, for example, begin to ask yourself what kind of house. What style is the exterior? Is it built of wood, bricks, or? How do the rooms flow from one to the other? Does the kitchen

Dr. Jill Ammon-Wexler

get morning light? In short, begin to build it in your mind's eye.

Just as world-level athletes create entirely new levels of performance, you can create whatever reality YOU desire. Science is solidly behind you!

⭐ Your mind is the ultimate success tool. All creativity, personal power, and success start in your physical brain. And YOU alone make the choice about how much of your brain's potential you will develop.

The power of your thoughts is beyond concept. You literally become what you think about. This now an accepted, scientifically-proven fact. All that remains is to put this to work in your life.

What Your Brain Does

Your amazing brain is far more than the simple stimulus-response machine it was once thought to be. It's actually the most dynamic, changeable organ of your entire body. In just the past few years, scientists have proven that your brain *constantly* alters itself to adapt to your circumstances.

We now know that each choice you make, each new thing you learn, instantly creates actual physical changes in your brain. Merely thinking about something brings about immediate physical changes in your brain.

At this very moment – as you read these words – your brain is making instant physical changes. Brand new neural connections are being created. And at the same time, old neural connections are being modified or eliminated.

Why Future Memories Work. Both actual vision and future memories stimulate two specific physical parts of the "thinking" portions of the brain – the prefrontal and frontal lobes of your cortex.

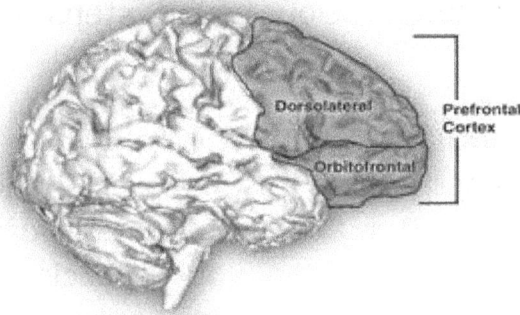

Your frontal and prefrontal lobes sit in the very front part of your brain, and are gigantic compared to the prefrontal lobes of other species. Why is this important? These two portions of your brain control your ability to:

- Be <u>aware</u> of what's going on around you,

- *Focus* your attention,

- *Anticipate* the consequences of your actions, and

- *Do several things at once* (drive in rush hour traffic while eating an apple and listening to a motivational tape).

Combined, these two parts of your brain allow you to create an image of something in the future and create actions to manifest it. In effect, this allows you to overcome the usual limits of time and space. Then your subconscious mind steps in and takes over.

Subconscious Mind Activities. When it comes to learning, most people assume we're talking about a conscious act. But actually your subconscious mind learns much more than your conscious mind, and does so effortlessly and automatically. Your subconscious mind *never* shuts down, and records everything you perceive, say or do whether you're awake or sleeping.

Understanding this helps you appreciate why our subconscious mind thinks very differently from our conscious mind.

First, your subconscious mind is NOT a logical thinking machine. It is creative, spontaneous, and totally illogical. If asked to explain what a dog is, your subconscious mind will be happy to respond with a scientific description of the animal "dog," an association of the word "dog" spelled backward (g-o-d), a picture of Snoopy, or even a memory of someone calling you a dog.

Second, it goes through such a creative association process nonstop 24 hours a day, and...

Third, your subconscious mind accepts *everything* you present to it as being of equal importance and reality. If you tell your subconscious mind that the "world is out to get you," it will treat this as being totally unquestioned reality and will encourage you to respond accordingly.

If on the other hand you inform your subconscious mind that the "world is on your side and supporting your dreams," it will treat this as a total unquestioned reality and will guide your actions accordingly.

In short, your subconscious mind is the source of your dreams, your hunches, your intuition, and all the inner messages that determine what you will (and will not) achieve in your life.

New Neural Networks. Suppose you have a dream or goal of creating the financial well being necessary to live your dream lifestyle. If you successfully build and focus on a future memory of having financial well being, you're actually using your brain to see yourself in the future having achieved this.

Then as you replay that future memory of being "well off," you create *very real* physical neural networks in your brain to support that vision. Then the more you focus on that future memory, the stronger and more stable those physical neural networks will become.

Plus something wonderful happens IF, at the same time, you also consciously refuse to pay attention on old negative memories. The neural networks holding those old memories then begin to lose the synaptic connections that glued them together.

Then if you refuse to give them attention long enough, they are eventually "pruned away" just like a gardener cuts off a dead branch. (This is solid modern neurological science, *not* a metaphor or imagined concept).

Accessing Your Subconscious. Your brain directly reflects your mental state in the form of electrical waves of energy known as brainwaves. If you are stressed, for example, your brain will emit very fast brainwaves in the high Beta and Gamma brainwave frequencies.

While if you are relaxed and enjoying a creative reverie, your brain will primarily emit Alpha brainwaves. The next slower brainwaves, Theta, are experienced while falling to sleep dreaming, or during deep meditation. The slowest brainwaves, Delta, are commonly produced during deep dreamless sleep.

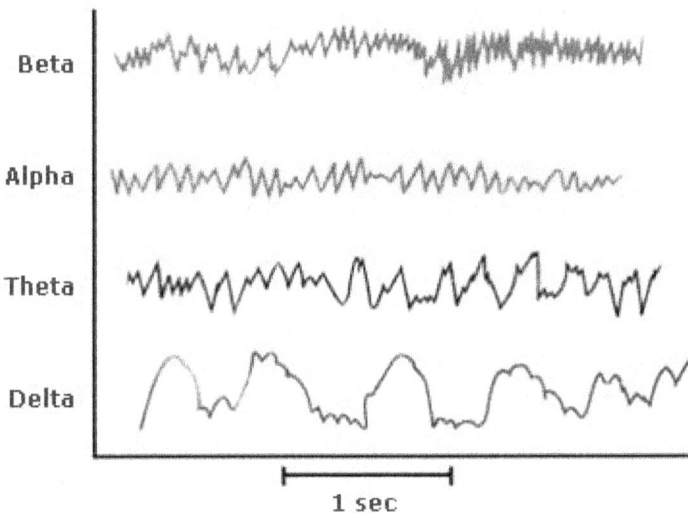

Beta

Alpha

Theta

Delta

1 sec

Taking Alpha Breaks. The important thing to note is that your thoughts and moods are <u>real</u>, and directly impact your brain. In terms of the goals of this book, a short Alpha break provides the instant

191

Dr. Jill Ammon-Wexler

physical and mental recharge that leads to the ability to create powerful future memories.

Actually a 10-minute Alpha session has the same positive effect of a 45-minute nap. Normally we automatically drop into Alpha several times a day, but it is very empowering to learn to do this on command.

If you are a meditator you have probably already developed this ability. If not an engineered Alpha brainwave training will get you there instantly.

Creating a Future Memory

Lasting transformations are never an accident or the result of luck. Success in any aspect of life is the result of a process:

- You decide what you want,

- You create and focus on a clear picture of exactly what it will look like when you get it, and

- You then begin to take consistent action to manifest your picture.

This process is used by all highly successful men and women – sometimes totally unconsciously – but its power is available to all. The better you get at

192

creating future memories, the faster you'll move toward achieving your dreams and goals.

How the Process Works

Let's return to our earlier example of having a dream or goal of improved financial well being. How can you create and use future memories to get you there?

Assuming you have a clear definition of what you desire ("financial well being"), your next step is to begin to create some very specific and detailed future memories of how it looks to have *already* achieved that dream or goal.

It's interesting to understand more about how this process works. First, it is NOT possible to create a future memory of such a vague concept as financial well being.

Future memories are a visualization-based process, and vision requires specific images. Such a "seeing" process requires that you clearly fill in the details of how it will be to have achieved that goal. The more detailed your picture of your dream or goal, the better you'll see and achieve it. Start here...

- What does this level of prosperity look like to you?

- What is your lifestyle like?

193

- What do you do each day?

- How do you live, and where?

- What car are you driving? What color is it? Does it have leather and a sunroof?

- What investments have you made? What kinds of stocks or properties? Who manages it for you?

- Who are your business associates and friends?

The KEY is to create some very clear and vivid pictures of what it looks like to have true financial well being.

Then it is absolutely necessary that you set aside some time each day to focus on your vision. If you fail to do this, the physical neural networks dedicated to your future memory will simply weaken, and will eventually be eliminated. (Remember the path through a meadow comparison?)

This is not theory. It's the scientifically-proven reality behind why people lose their vision and just give up on their dreams. The physical law that applies to your brain's neural networks is the same physical law that applies to muscles: Use it, or lose it!

Future memories are real, and YOU are the creative force behind them! So – what do you want in your life?

What is your vision of what you want to manifest? Once you have clarified your vision, create a clear future memory, commit to it, and go to work manifesting it. Your level of confidence will build as you build those physical neurons. Get ready for some amazing things to happen in your life! Your mind is the ultimate tool for success.

Build Mental Focus

An important tool for achieving your dream lifestyle is to discipline yourself to think and talk only about only what you want – *not* about what you *don't* want. Discipline yourself to refuse to focus or talk about anything you don't want.

Many people have not committed to creating mental discipline. Instead of focusing on what they want in their lives, their mental focus wanders. One minute they contemplate a wonderful dream, but in the next minute they focus on a powerful mental picture of a past failure to achieve it.

A far better approach is this: No matter what's happening, keep your attention on your dreams and related goals! If you have financial problems, refuse to focus on them. Remember: What you focus on, gains strength in your brain's neural networks. If a negative thought comes into your mind, push it out! Get your mind back on what you *want.*

If you do this, soon you will find yourself thinking about your dreams and related goals most of the time. And that's one of the attributes of the world's most successful people.

As you think about your desired lifestyle, your subconscious mind will automatically direct your actions and thoughts toward creating it. Since your subconscious mind can't tell the difference between a vividly imagined future memory and an outside reality, your desire puts your subconscious mind on your side.

For example, suppose you go to the Mercedes dealership and take your dream model for a drive. And as you drive along you create a future memory of owning that Mercedes. If you accompany that future memory with the feelings of joy that go along with driving that beautiful machine, your subconscious mind will simply accept that the Mercedes is yours.

Your subconscious mind will then go to work. It will urge you to do the things that will make it possible for you to actually own that Mercedes.

☆ Used properly, your future memories will move you toward your dreams and supporting goals faster than any other success method.

Powering-Up Future Memories

Here are some suggestions on powering-up your future memories for faster positive results:

Build Clarity. The more clearly and completely you can "see" something you want, the more rapidly you will materialize it. Many, many people do NOT have a clear picture of their dreams. They may say they want financial freedom or happiness, but can't describe what that would actually mean to them.

You need vivid clarity and details in your future memories. The more time you invest creating detailed mental pictures of having already achieved your dream and supporting goals, the more rapidly those pictures will be accepted by your subconscious mind as actual instructions to be followed!

Use Emotional Intensity. The intensity of your future memories depends upon the emotional intensity of your desire. If you attach intense desire to a future memory, it is burned into your subconscious mind (and your neural networks) as a directive.

Dr. Jill Ammon-Wexler

Emotion is a major key to the creation of effective future memories. By itself, thought has very little influence over your powerful subconscious mind. But if you combine your thought of financial well being with the emotional excitement of driving that desired Mercedes, then you have real power to push you forward toward your goals.

Emotion is the raw energy that drives you to DO the things that will make your future memory a reality. So DO get excited. Move forward toward your goal by creating clear future memories of what it looks like to be there, and feel the emotional high that goes along with it.

Put Repetition to Work. When you first begin to create a future memory of having accomplished something entirely new, your subconscious mind will likely respond with some resistance. Your new future memory is creating dissonance in your subconscious mind. It is challenging older embedded memories of perhaps failing to achieve what you're after.

The way to override those old memories is to revisit and repeat your emotion-packed future memories again and again, until you have strengthened those *new* neural networks.

Do NOT Worry. Worrying is an especially powerful form of *negative* goal setting. When you worry, you create emotion-packed future memories of having something you do not want. Your subconscious mind will push you toward creating your future memories, so avoid worry. It will bring you exactly what you're worried about!

Some Reminders

Here are a few things you'll want to remember about creating future memories:

-It does NOT matter that what you're picturing as a future memory is NOT "real" yet!

-Future memories are NOT just daydreams. They create the actual physical neural networks that your future reality will be based on.

-The more often you focus on your future memories, the more complex your future memory neural networks will become. This increased brain complexity leads to highly creative "whole brain thinking."

-Your subconscious mind CANNOT tell the difference between something you physically "see," and something you mentally picture as a "future memory." And this powerful part of your mind runs 24 hours a day, 7 days a week – even when your

Dr. Jill Ammon-Wexler

conscious mind is asleep or distracted with something else.

-Your subconscious mind is the source of the internal messages that program your actions, and largely determines what you will (or will not) manage to achieve in your life.

- -

TWELVE. THE POWER OF WORDS

Few of us realize how powerful our words can be. The words we use to state our intent <u>reveal</u> whether we will (or will not) actually reach our dream or goal. How can this be so? Our choice of words is never random. Our choices not only reflect our mental state, they also guide our resulting actions and reactions.

A "Guaranteed-Failure" Statement

Let's say you're fired-up to create some exciting lasting change in your life. You've set your dream or goal down on paper, and even created a plan of action to achieve it. You've got fire and desire, and you know exactly what you're going to do. You promise yourself, "Starting tomorrow

I'll try to—" You just took a crippling misstep before you even started, and it will ensure you will NOT achieve that dream or goal. What do the words "I'll

Dr. Jill Ammon-Wexler

try" really mean? They indicate you've given yourself an exit, just in case you hit some bumps in the road.

The word try lacks intention and confidence. It assumes failure. It says, "Alright, I'll give it a go, but I do not expect to succeed." Try provides a built-in escape route and guarantees almost certain failure.

An "Over the Rainbow" Statement

Now let's see how it feels to use an "I am" statement. Suppose your dream or goal is to feel better by reaching your ideal weight. You could use the "I am" statement to tell yourself something like: "I am going to feel better by walking 20 minutes a day, 5 days a week."

"I am" at least does not presume failure. But there's still a problem when you say "I am."

The problem? When and where are you going to take your intended action? This statement, although an improvement, does *not* reflect a specific commitment to take action.

If you find you're having trouble committing to when and where, it may be time to take a good look at either your dream or goal, or your plan to manifest it. If your dream or goal is right, maybe your plan has you starting at the wrong first step.

Back up and identify a simple action you're ready to take NOW. It doesn't matter how small it may seem. You're often better off starting with a small step and achieving success – as opposed to starting off with a huge step you're not ready to handle.

Success, no matter how small, builds your ability to realize more success!

A "NOW" Statement. Once you've refined your starting point, now notice how it feels like to say: "I am now..." This statement establishes a sense of power and intention. It says you truly mean business. That you believe in what you are saying, and you are right *NOW* taking a step to make it happen.

It indicates you are in action and have made a very real commitment to yourself you are NOW honouring. It also says that you WILL find a way to manifest your dream, even if there are bumps in the road.

Higher levels of success reaching dreams and goals depends on: (1) Coming from the most passionate place within yourself, (2) Focusing on a clear vision of how it feels to have *already* achieved that dream, (3) Breaking your dream down into a series of small easily achievable steps, and (4) Committing to take each action step one at a time starting NOW!

Dr. Jill Ammon-Wexler

Think about it – we really can *only* do what is before us right now! Tomorrow's larger success and happiness is built on today's smaller successes. This "NOW" approach makes your dream or goal success inevitable.

OK, here's the BIG question: *When* are you going to *commit* to DO what you need to do to reach your dream or goal?

Take Action

Harnessing the power of your mind to create your dream lifestyle is a truly exhilarating experience. It all starts with a decision. That only takes a millisecond of time.

There's no time like NOW to clarify and state your greatest goal. Be as specific and detailed as possible, use the power of future memories, and take consistent action every day to move toward your dreams and goals. Enjoy the journey!

Dr Jill Ammon-Wexler

WANT MORE?

AMAZE YOURSELF:

Take a Quantum Leap

Another of Dr. Jill's popular books continues where you just left off with this book. Read this book to supercharge your confidence, light up your creativity, start to feel great every day, take control of your stress, enter the flow, stop mental aging, and much more.

http://www.amazon.com/dp/B0073V7VOM

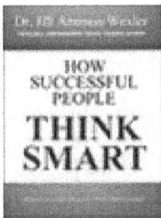

OTHER BOOKS AND PROGRAMS

Information about the author's other books and programs is available here =>
http://www.BuildMindPower.com

Dr. Jill Ammon-Wexler

Ready for the Next Step? SERIOUS about supercharging your life? The author is a world renowned neuro-psychologist and brain/mind research pioneer. Her unique collection of down-loadable MP3 brainwave trainings will help you create truly efffective future memories. This special collection of stereo-quality MP3s is valued at $52.80, but is only $19.95 for you, as a book buyer => **http://www.QuantumLeapAudios.com**

Want to Go Deeper?
Are **YOU** one of those special people with a deep passionate desire to accomplish more in your life? If so ... Dr. Ammon-Wexler would like to personally invite you to come participate in her unique QUANTUM MIND TRAINING PROGRAM.

Come develop and refine your brain/mind power at your convenience and in the comfort of your own home....

The exciting 3-month **Quantum Mind** program is packed with unique training audios, videos, and specially engineered brainwave training.

The end results include greatly increased creativity, focus, intelligence, total stress management, mental clarity, and remarkably superior levels of brain/mind performance. Open up your natural genius and tap into higher, more valuable states of awareness and consciousness.

Go learn more and take advantage of a temporary deep book buyer's discount =>

http://www.HotBrainz.com

Dr. Jill Ammon-Wexler

ABOUT THE AUTHOR

Author, Dr. Jill Ammon-Wexler is a doctor of psychology, pioneer brain/mind researcher, committed life adventurer, and the author of over 30 books, hundreds of articles and research reports, and several popular personal empowerment training programs.

She founded California's Human Dynamics Workshop and the InnerSpace Center, where she conducted Esalen-inspired intensive workshops and mind power training. Her mentors have included: Angeles Arien, Gia Fu-Feng, Soygal Rinpoche, Sri Anandi Ma, Abraham Maslow, Jay McCullough, Jacob Moreno, Virginia Satir, Bruce Ogilvie, Fritz Perls, Alan Watts and many other unique experts.

Her special pursuits include home design and remodeling, gardening, being out of doors, skiing, working toward higher states of consciousness, art painting, and making a positive difference in the lives of her readers and students. You can explore her brainwave training collections, audio books, printed and Kindle books and training programs here=>
http://www.BuildMindPower.com

www.ingramcontent.com/pod-product-compliance
Lightning Source LLC
Chambersburg PA
CBHW070955040426
42443CB00007B/512